Human rights today:
European legal texts

Council of Europe Publishing

French edition:

Les droits de l'homme: repères juridiques européens

ISBN 92-871-3812-5

Cover design: Graphic Design Workshop of the Council of Europe

Council of Europe Publishing
F-67075 Strasbourg Cedex

ISBN 92-871-3813-3
© Council of Europe, January 1999
Printed in Germany

Contents

Preface

This is the second edition of a collection originally entitled *European Convention on Human Rights: Collected texts*, which was first published in 1994.

In the few years that have elapsed since this first publication, there have been several important developments in the field of human rights protection. In 1994, Protocol No. 11 to the European Convention on Human Rights was opened for signature; on 1 November 1998 it entered into force. Under the provisions of this protocol the European Court of Human Rights is henceforth a permanent body, to which both individuals and states have the right to bring applications concerning complaints against States Parties to the Convention. The European Convention on Human Rights, as amended, is included in this volume, together with the explanatory memorandum to Protocol No. 11.

But there is a growing perception that human rights protection is not limited to the areas covered by the European Convention on Human Rights. The European Convention for the Prevention of Torture and Inhuman or Degrading Treatment or Punishment has been in force for almost ten years. It provides for the setting up of an international committee empowered to visit all places where persons are deprived of their liberty by a public authority. The committee, composed of independent experts, may make recommendations and suggest improvements, in order to strengthen, if necessary, the protection of persons visited from torture and from inhuman or degrading treatment or punishment. This preventive, non-judicial machinery is an important addition to the system of protection already existing under the European Convention on Human Rights.

A new instrument drawn up since the publication of the original version of this book is the Framework Convention for the Protection of National Minorities. This is the first legally binding multilateral instrument concerned with the protection of national minorities in general. Its aim is to protect the existence of national minorities within the respective territories of the Parties. The convention seeks to promote the full and effective equality of national minorities by creating appropriate conditions enabling them to preserve and develop their culture and to retain their identity. It sets out principles relating to persons belonging to national minorities in the sphere of public life, such as freedom of peaceful assembly, freedom of association, freedom of expression, freedom of thought, conscience and religion, and access to the media, as well as in the sphere of freedoms relating to language, education, transfrontier co-operation, etc. The convention entered into force in February 1998.

In the field of social rights the European Social Charter continues to set standards. The Charter, its protocols, the revised Charter and other important references concerning its application and the associated procedures are published in a companion volume.[1]

A further consideration is the expansion of the Council of Europe in the 1990s to encompass almost all European states. Eight out of the forty member states joined the Council between 1994 and 1998. Such rapid changes, together with the wide variety of national histories, economic situations and social environments, may be seen to place an extra burden on the bodies responsible for enforcing the human rights instruments and for monitoring member states' commitments; but at the same time this very diversity is a source of strength to the protection machinery, and to the Organisation responsible for it.

I am sure that this new edition of collected texts, with its expanded scope, will deserve a place in the reference library of all concerned with the protection of human rights.

Daniel Tarschys
Secretary General of the Council of Europe

---

1. *European Social Charter: collected texts* (Council of Europe Publishing, 1997, ISBN 92-871-3366-2).

European Convention
on Human Rights

and related texts

Convention for the Protection of Human Rights and Fundamental Freedoms
(European Treaty Series, No. 5)
as amended by Protocol No. 11

Rome, 4.XI.1950

The text of the Convention had been amended according to the provisions of Protocol No. 3 (ETS No. 45), which entered into force on 21 September 1970, of Protocol No. 5 (ETS No. 55), which entered into force on 20 December 1971 and of Protocol No. 8 (ETS No. 118), which entered into force on 1 January 1990, and comprised also the text of Protocol No. 2 (ETS No. 44) which, in accordance with Article 5, paragraph 3 thereof, had been an integral part of the Convention since its entry into force on 21 September 1970. All provisions which had been amended or added by these Protocols are replaced by Protocol No. 11 (ETS No. 55), as from the date of its entry into force on 1 November 1998. As from that date, Protocol No. 9 (ETS No. 140), which entered into force on 1 October 1994, is repealed.

The governments signatory hereto, being members of the Council of Europe,

Considering the Universal Declaration of Human Rights proclaimed by the General Assembly of the United Nations on 10th December 1948;

Considering that this Declaration aims at securing the universal and effective recognition and observance of the Rights therein declared;

Considering that the aim of the Council of Europe is the achievement of greater unity between its members and that one of the methods by which that aim is to be pursued is the maintenance and further realisation of human rights and fundamental freedoms;

Reaffirming their profound belief in those fundamental freedoms which are the foundation of justice and peace in the world and are best maintained on the one hand by an effective political democracy and on the other by a common understanding and observance of the human rights upon which they depend;

Being resolved, as the governments of European countries which are like-minded and have a common heritage of political traditions, ideals, freedom and the rule of law, to take the first steps for the collective enforcement of certain of the rights stated in the Universal Declaration,

Have agreed as follows:

Article 1[1] – Obligation to respect human rights

The High Contracting Parties shall secure to everyone within their jurisdiction the rights and freedoms defined in Section I of this Convention.

Section I – Rights and freedoms

Article 2[1] – Right to life

1 Everyone's right to life shall be protected by law. No one shall be deprived of his life intentionally save in the execution of a sentence of a court following his conviction of a crime for which this penalty is provided by law.

2 Deprivation of life shall not be regarded as inflicted in contravention of this article when it results from the use of force which is no more than absolutely necessary:

   a in defence of any person from unlawful violence;

   b in order to effect a lawful arrest or to prevent the escape of a person lawfully detained;

   c in action lawfully taken for the purpose of quelling a riot or insurrection.

Article 3[1] – Prohibition of torture

No one shall be subjected to torture or to inhuman or degrading treatment or punishment.

Article 4[1] – Prohibition of slavery and forced labour

1 No one shall be held in slavery or servitude.

2 No one shall be required to perform forced or compulsory labour.

3 For the purpose of this article the term "forced or compulsory labour" shall not include:

   a any work required to be done in the ordinary course of detention imposed according to the provisions of Article 5 of this Convention or during conditional release from such detention;

   b any service of a military character or, in case of conscientious objectors in countries where they are recognised, service exacted instead of compulsory military service;

   c any service exacted in case of an emergency or calamity threatening the life or well-being of the community;

   d any work or service which forms part of normal civic obligations.

---

1. Heading added according to the provisions of Protocol No. 11 (ETS No. 155).

Article 5[1] – Right to liberty and security

1 Everyone has the right to liberty and security of person. No one shall be deprived of his liberty save in the following cases and in accordance with a procedure prescribed by law:

   a the lawful detention of a person after conviction by a competent court;

   b the lawful arrest or detention of a person for non- compliance with the lawful order of a court or in order to secure the fulfilment of any obligation prescribed by law;

   c the lawful arrest or detention of a person effected for the purpose of bringing him before the competent legal authority on reasonable suspicion of having committed an offence or when it is reasonably considered necessary to prevent his committing an offence or fleeing after having done so;

   d the detention of a minor by lawful order for the purpose of educational supervision or his lawful detention for the purpose of bringing him before the competent legal authority;

   e the lawful detention of persons for the prevention of the spreading of infectious diseases, of persons of unsound mind, alcoholics or drug addicts or vagrants;

   f the lawful arrest or detention of a person to prevent his effecting an unauthorised entry into the country or of a person against whom action is being taken with a view to deportation or extradition.

2 Everyone who is arrested shall be informed promptly, in a language which he understands, of the reasons for his arrest and of any charge against him.

3 Everyone arrested or detained in accordance with the provisions of paragraph 1.c of this article shall be brought promptly before a judge or other officer authorised by law to exercise judicial power and shall be entitled to trial within a reasonable time or to release pending trial. Release may be conditioned by guarantees to appear for trial.

4 Everyone who is deprived of his liberty by arrest or detention shall be entitled to take proceedings by which the lawfulness of his detention shall be decided speedily by a court and his release ordered if the detention is not lawful.

5 Everyone who has been the victim of arrest or detention in contravention of the provisions of this article shall have an enforceable right to compensation.

---

1. Heading added according to the provisions of Protocol No. 11 (ETS No. 155).

Article 6[1] – Right to a fair trial

1 In the determination of his civil rights and obligations or of any criminal charge against him, everyone is entitled to a fair and public hearing within a reasonable time by an independent and impartial tribunal established by law. Judgment shall be pronounced publicly but the press and public may be excluded from all or part of the trial in the interests of morals, public order or national security in a democratic society, where the interests of juveniles or the protection of the private life of the parties so require, or to the extent strictly necessary in the opinion of the court in special circumstances where publicity would prejudice the interests of justice.

2 Everyone charged with a criminal offence shall be presumed innocent until proved guilty according to law.

3 Everyone charged with a criminal offence has the following minimum rights:

a to be informed promptly, in a language which he understands and in detail, of the nature and cause of the accusation against him;

b to have adequate time and facilities for the preparation of his defence;

c to defend himself in person or through legal assistance of his own choosing or, if he has not sufficient means to pay for legal assistance, to be given it free when the interests of justice so require;

d to examine or have examined witnesses against him and to obtain the attendance and examination of witnesses on his behalf under the same conditions as witnesses against him;

e to have the free assistance of an interpreter if he cannot understand or speak the language used in court.

Article 7[1] – No punishment without law

1 No one shall be held guilty of any criminal offence on account of any act or omission which did not constitute a criminal offence under national or international law at the time when it was committed. Nor shall a heavier penalty be imposed than the one that was applicable at the time the criminal offence was committed.

2 This article shall not prejudice the trial and punishment of any person for any act or omission which, at the time when it was committed, was criminal according to the general principles of law recognised by civilised nations.

---

1. Heading added according to the provisions of Protocol No. 11 (ETS No. 155).

Article 8[1] – Right to respect for private and family life

1 Everyone has the right to respect for his private and family life, his home and his correspondence.

2 There shall be no interference by a public authority with the exercise of this right except such as is in accordance with the law and is necessary in a democratic society in the interests of national security, public safety or the economic well-being of the country, for the prevention of disorder or crime, for the protection of health or morals, or for the protection of the rights and freedoms of others.

Article 9[1] – Freedom of thought, conscience and religion

1 Everyone has the right to freedom of thought, conscience and religion; this right includes freedom to change his religion or belief and freedom, either alone or in community with others and in public or private, to manifest his religion or belief, in worship, teaching, practice and observance.

2 Freedom to manifest one's religion or beliefs shall be subject only to such limitations as are prescribed by law and are necessary in a democratic society in the interests of public safety, for the protection of public order, health or morals, or for the protection of the rights and freedoms of others.

Article 10[1] – Freedom of expression

1 Everyone has the right to freedom of expression. This right shall include freedom to hold opinions and to receive and impart information and ideas without interference by public authority and regardless of frontiers. This article shall not prevent States from requiring the licensing of broadcasting, television or cinema enterprises.

2 The exercise of these freedoms, since it carries with it duties and responsibilities, may be subject to such formalities, conditions, restrictions or penalties as are prescribed by law and are necessary in a democratic society, in the interests of national security, territorial integrity or public safety, for the prevention of disorder or crime, for the protection of health or morals, for the protection of the reputation or rights of others, for preventing the disclosure of information received in confidence, or for maintaining the authority and impartiality of the judiciary.

Article 11[1] – Freedom of assembly and association

1 Everyone has the right to freedom of peaceful assembly and to freedom of association with others, including the right to form and to join trade unions for the protection of his interests.

---

1. Heading added according to the provisions of Protocol No. 11 (ETS No. 155).

2 No restrictions shall be placed on the exercise of these rights other than such as are prescribed by law and are necessary in a democratic society in the interests of national security or public safety, for the prevention of disorder or crime, for the protection of health or morals or for the protection of the rights and freedoms of others. This article shall not prevent the imposition of lawful restrictions on the exercise of these rights by members of the armed forces, of the police or of the administration of the State.

Article 12[1] – Right to marry

Men and women of marriageable age have the right to marry and to found a family, according to the national laws governing the exercise of this right.

Article 13[1] – Right to an effective remedy

Everyone whose rights and freedoms as set forth in this Convention are violated shall have an effective remedy before a national authority notwithstanding that the violation has been committed by persons acting in an official capacity.

Article 14[1] – Prohibition of discrimination

The enjoyment of the rights and freedoms set forth in this Convention shall be secured without discrimination on any ground such as sex, race, colour, language, religion, political or other opinion, national or social origin, association with a national minority, property, birth or other status.

Article 15[1] – Derogation in time of emergency

1 In time of war or other public emergency threatening the life of the nation any High Contracting Party may take measures derogating from its obligations under this Convention to the extent strictly required by the exigencies of the situation, provided that such measures are not inconsistent with its other obligations under international law.

2 No derogation from Article 2, except in respect of deaths resulting from lawful acts of war, or from Articles 3, 4 (paragraph 1) and 7 shall be made under this provision.

3 Any High Contracting Party availing itself of this right of derogation shall keep the Secretary General of the Council of Europe fully informed of the measures which it has taken and the reasons therefor. It shall also inform the Secretary General of the Council of Europe when such measures have ceased to operate and the provisions of the Convention are again being fully executed.

---

1. Heading added according to the provisions of Protocol No. 11 (ETS No. 155).

Article 16[1] – Restrictions on political activity of aliens

Nothing in Articles 10, 11 and 14 shall be regarded as preventing the High Contracting Parties from imposing restrictions on the political activity of aliens.

Article 17[1] – Prohibition of abuse of rights

Nothing in this Convention may be interpreted as implying for any State, group or person any right to engage in any activity or perform any act aimed at the destruction of any of the rights and freedoms set forth herein or at their limitation to a greater extent than is provided for in the Convention.

Article 18[1] – Limitation on use of restrictions on rights

The restrictions permitted under this Convention to the said rights and freedoms shall not be applied for any purpose other than those for which they have been prescribed.

Section II[2] – European Court of Human Rights

Article 19 – Establishment of the Court

To ensure the observance of the engagements undertaken by the High Contracting Parties in the Convention and the Protocols thereto, there shall be set up a European Court of Human Rights, hereinafter referred to as "the Court". It shall function on a permanent basis.

Article 20 – Number of judges

The Court shall consist of a number of judges equal to that of the High Contracting Parties.

Article 21 – Criteria for office

1 The judges shall be of high moral character and must either possess the qualifications required for appointment to high judicial office or be jurisconsults of recognised competence.

2 The judges shall sit on the Court in their individual capacity.

3 During their term of office the judges shall not engage in any activity which is incompatible with their independence, impartiality or with the demands of a full-time office; all questions arising from the application of this paragraph shall be decided by the Court.

---

1. Heading added according to the provisions of Protocol No. 11 (ETS No. 155).
2. Text amended in accordance with the provisions of Protocol No. 11 (ETS No. 155).

Article 22 – Election of judges

1 The judges shall be elected by the Parliamentary Assembly with respect to each High Contracting Party by a majority of votes cast from a list of three candidates nominated by the High Contracting Party.

2 The same procedure shall be followed to complete the Court in the event of the accession of new High Contracting Parties and in filling casual vacancies.

Article 23 – Terms of office

1 The judges shall be elected for a period of six years. They may be re-elected. However, the terms of office of one-half of the judges elected at the first election shall expire at the end of three years.

2 The judges whose terms of office are to expire at the end of the initial period of three years shall be chosen by lot by the Secretary General of the Council of Europe immediately after their election.

3 In order to ensure that, as far as possible, the terms of office of one-half of the judges are renewed every three years, the Parliamentary Assembly may decide, before proceeding to any subsequent election, that the term or terms of office of one or more judges to be elected shall be for a period other than six years but not more than nine and not less than three years.

4 In cases where more than one term of office is involved and where the Parliamentary Assembly applies the preceding paragraph, the allocation of the terms of office shall be effected by a drawing of lots by the Secretary General of the Council of Europe immediately after the election.

5 A judge elected to replace a judge whose term of office has not expired shall hold office for the remainder of his predecessor's term.

6 The terms of office of judges shall expire when they reach the age of 70.

7 The judges shall hold office until replaced. They shall, however, continue to deal with such cases as they already have under consideration.

Article 24 – Dismissal

No judge may be dismissed from his office unless the other judges decide by a majority of two-thirds that he has ceased to fulfil the required conditions.

Article 25 – Registry and legal secretaries

The Court shall have a registry, the functions and organisation of which shall be laid down in the rules of the Court. The Court shall be assisted by legal secretaries.

Article 26 – Plenary Court

The plenary Court shall

    a elect its President and one or two Vice-Presidents for a period of three years; they may be re-elected;

    b set up Chambers, constituted for a fixed period of time;

    c elect the Presidents of the Chambers of the Court; they may be re-elected;

    d adopt the rules of the Court, and

    e elect the Registrar and one or more Deputy Registrars.

Article 27 – Committees, Chambers and Grand Chamber

1 To consider cases brought before it, the Court shall sit in committees of three judges, in Chambers of seven judges and in a Grand Chamber of seventeen judges. The Court's Chambers shall set up committees for a fixed period of time.

2 There shall sit as an ex officio member of the Chamber and the Grand Chamber the judge elected in respect of the State Party concerned or, if there is none or if he is unable to sit, a person of its choice who shall sit in the capacity of judge.

3 The Grand Chamber shall also include the President of the Court, the Vice-Presidents, the Presidents of the Chambers and other judges chosen in accordance with the rules of the Court. When a case is referred to the Grand Chamber under Article 43, no judge from the Chamber which rendered the judgment shall sit in the Grand Chamber, with the exception of the President of the Chamber and the judge who sat in respect of the State Party concerned.

Article 28 – Declarations of inadmissibility by committees

A committee may, by a unanimous vote, declare inadmissible or strike out of its list of cases an application submitted under Article 34 where such a decision can be taken without further examination. The decision shall be final.

Article 29 – Decisions by Chambers on admissibility and merits

1 If no decision is taken under Article 28, a Chamber shall decide on the admissibility and merits of individual applications submitted under Article 34.

2 A Chamber shall decide on the admissibility and merits of inter-State applications submitted under Article 33.

3 The decision on admissibility shall be taken separately unless the Court, in exceptional cases, decides otherwise.

Article 30 – Relinquishment of jurisdiction to the Grand Chamber

Where a case pending before a Chamber raises a serious question affecting the interpretation of the Convention or the protocols thereto, or where the resolution of a question before the Chamber might have a result inconsistent with a judgment previously delivered by the Court, the Chamber may, at any time before it has rendered its judgment, relinquish jurisdiction in favour of the Grand Chamber, unless one of the parties to the case objects.

Article 31 – Powers of the Grand Chamber

The Grand Chamber shall

    a   determine applications submitted either under Article 33 or Article 34 when a Chamber has relinquished jurisdiction under Article 30 or when the case has been referred to it under Article 43 ; and

    b   consider requests for advisory opinions submitted under Article 47.

Article 32 – Jurisdiction of the Court

1   The jurisdiction of the Court shall extend to all matters concerning the interpretation and application of the Convention and the protocols thereto which are referred to it as provided in Articles 33, 34 and 47.

2   In the event of dispute as to whether the Court has jurisdiction, the Court shall decide.

Article 33 – Inter-State cases

Any High Contracting Party may refer to the Court any alleged breach of the provisions of the Convention and the protocols thereto by another High Contracting Party.

Article 34 – Individual applications

The Court may receive applications from any person, non-governmental organisation or group of individuals claiming to be the victim of a violation by one of the High Contracting Parties of the rights set forth in the Convention or the protocols thereto. The High Contracting Parties undertake not to hinder in any way the effective exercise of this right.

Article 35 – Admissibility criteria

1   The Court may only deal with the matter after all domestic remedies have been exhausted, according to the generally recognised rules of international law, and within a period of six months from the date on which the final decision was taken.

2   The Court shall not deal with any application submitted under Article 34 that

a   is anonymous; or

b   is substantially the same as a matter that has already been examined by the Court or has already been submitted to another procedure of international investigation or settlement and contains no relevant new information.

3   The Court shall declare inadmissible any individual application submitted under Article 34 which it considers incompatible with the provisions of the Convention or the protocols thereto, manifestly ill-founded, or an abuse of the right of application.

4   The Court shall reject any application which it considers inadmissible under this Article. It may do so at any stage of the proceedings.

Article 36 – Third party intervention

1   In all cases before a Chamber of the Grand Chamber, a High Contracting Party one of whose nationals is an applicant shall have the right to submit written comments and to take part in hearings.

2   The President of the Court may, in the interest of the proper administration of justice, invite any High Contracting Party which is not a party to the proceedings or any person concerned who is not the applicant to submit written comments or take part in hearings.

Article 37 – Striking out applications

1   The Court may at any stage of the proceedings decide to strike an application out of its list of cases where the circumstances lead to the conclusion that

a   the applicant does not intend to pursue his application; or

b   the matter has been resolved; or

c   for any other reason established by the Court, it is no longer justified to continue the examination of the application.

However, the Court shall continue the examination of the application if respect for human rights as defined in the Convention and the protocols thereto so requires.

2   The Court may decide to restore an application to its list of cases if it considers that the circumstances justify such a course.

Article 38 – Examination of the case and friendly settlement proceedings

1   If the Court declares the application admissible, it shall

a   pursue the examination of the case, together with the representatives of the parties, and if need be, undertake an investigation, for the effective conduct of which the States concerned shall furnish all necessary facilities;

b place itself at the disposal of the parties concerned with a view to securing a friendly settlement of the matter on the basis of respect for human rights as defined in the Convention and the protocols thereto.

2 Proceedings conducted under paragraph 1.b shall be confidential.

Article 39 – Finding of a friendly settlement

If a friendly settlement is effected, the Court shall strike the case out of its list by means of a decision which shall be confined to a brief statement of the facts and of the solution reached.

Article 40 – Public hearings and access to documents

1 Hearings shall be in public unless the Court in exceptional circumstances decides otherwise.

2 Documents deposited with the Registrar shall be accessible to the public unless the President of the Court decides otherwise.

Article 41 – Just satisfaction

If the Court finds that there has been a violation of the Convention or the protocols thereto, and if the internal law of the High Contracting Party concerned allows only partial reparation to be made, the Court shall, if necessary, afford just satisfaction to the injured party.

Article 42 – Judgments of Chambers

Judgments of Chambers shall become final in accordance with the provisions of Article 44, paragraph 2.

Article 43 – Referral to the Grand Chamber

1 Within a period of three months from the date of the judgment of the Chamber, any party to the case may, in exceptional cases, request that the case be referred to the Grand Chamber.

2 A panel of five judges of the Grand Chamber shall accept the request if the case raises a serious question affecting the interpretation or application of the Convention or the protocols thereto, or a serious issue of general importance.

3 If the panel accepts the request, the Grand Chamber shall decide the case by means of a judgment.

Article 44 – Final judgments

1   The judgment of the Grand Chamber shall be final.

2   The judgment of a Chamber shall become final

    a   when the parties declare that they will not request that the case be referred to the Grand Chamber; or

    b   three months after the date of the judgment, if reference of the case to the Grand Chamber has not been requested; or

    c   when the panel of the Grand Chamber rejects the request to refer under Article 43.

3   The final judgment shall be published.

Article 45 – Reasons for judgments and decisions

1   Reasons shall be given for judgments as well as for decisions declaring applications admissible or inadmissible.

2   If a judgment does not represent, in whole or in part, the unanimous opinion of the judges, any judge shall be entitled to deliver a separate opinion.

Article 46 – Binding force and execution of judgments

1   The High Contracting Parties undertake to abide by the final judgment of the Court in any case to which they are parties.

2   The final judgment of the Court shall be transmitted to the Committee of Ministers, which shall supervise its execution.

Article 47 – Advisory opinions

1   The Court may, at the request of the Committee of Ministers, give advisory opinions on legal questions concerning the interpretation of the Convention and the protocols thereto.

2   Such opinions shall not deal with any question relating to the content or scope of the rights or freedoms defined in Section I of the Convention and the protocols thereto, or with any other question which the Court or the Committee of Ministers might have to consider in consequence of any such proceedings as could be instituted in accordance with the Convention.

3   Decisions of the Committee of Ministers to request an advisory opinion of the Court shall require a majority vote of the representatives entitled to sit on the Committee.

Article 48 – Advisory jurisdiction of the Court

The Court shall decide whether a request for an advisory opinion submitted by the Committee of Ministers is within its competence as defined in Article 47.

Article 49 – Reasons for advisory opinions

1 Reasons shall be given for advisory opinions of the Court.

2 If the advisory opinion does not represent, in whole or in part, the unanimous opinion of the judges, any judge shall be entitled to deliver a separate opinion.

3 Advisory opinions of the Court shall be communicated to the Committee of Ministers.

Article 50 – Expenditure on the Court

The expenditure on the Court shall be borne by the Council of Europe.

Article 51 – Privileges and immunities of judges

The judges shall be entitled, during the exercise of their functions, to the privileges and immunities provided for in Article 40 of the Statute of the Council of Europe and in the agreements made thereunder.

Section III[1,2] – Miscellaneous provisions

Article 52[1] – Inquiries by the Secretary General

On receipt of a request from the Secretary General of the Council of Europe any High Contracting Party shall furnish an explanation of the manner in which its internal law ensures the effective implementation of any of the provisions of the Convention.

Article 53[1] – Safeguard for existing human rights

Nothing in this Convention shall be construed as limiting or derogating from any of the human rights and fundamental freedoms which may be ensured under the laws of any High Contracting Party or under any other agreement to which it is a Party.

Article 54[1] – Powers of the Committee of Ministers

Nothing in this Convention shall prejudice the powers conferred on the Committee of Ministers by the Statute of the Council of Europe.

---

1. Heading added according to the provisions of Protocol No. 11 (ETS No. 155).
2. The articles of this section are renumbered in accordance with the provisions of Protocol No. 11 (ETS No. 155).

Article 55[1] – Exclusion of other means of dispute settlement

The High Contracting Parties agree that, except by special agreement, they will not avail themselves of treaties, conventions or declarations in force between them for the purpose of submitting, by way of petition, a dispute arising out of the interpretation or application of this Convention to a means of settlement other than those provided for in this Convention.

Article 56[1] – Territorial application

1[2] Any State may at the time of its ratification or at any time thereafter declare by notification addressed to the Secretary General of the Council of Europe that the present Convention shall, subject to paragraph 4 of this Article, extend to all or any of the territories for whose international relations it is responsible.

2 The Convention shall extend to the territory or territories named in the notification as from the thirtieth day after the receipt of this notification by the Secretary General of the Council of Europe.

3 The provisions of this Convention shall be applied in such territories with due regard, however, to local requirements.

4[2] Any State which has made a declaration in accordance with paragraph 1 of this article may at any time thereafter declare on behalf of one or more of the territories to which the declaration relates that it accepts the competence of the Court to receive applications from individuals, non-governmental organisations or groups of individuals as provided by Article 34 of the Convention.

Article 57[1] – Reservations

1 Any State may, when signing this Convention or when depositing its instrument of ratification, make a reservation in respect of any particular provision of the Convention to the extent that any law then in force in its territory is not in conformity with the provision. Reservations of a general character shall not be permitted under this article.

2 Any reservation made under this article shall contain a brief statement of the law concerned.

Article 58[1] – Denunciation

1 A High Contracting Party may denounce the present Convention only after the expiry of five years from the date on which it became a party to it and after six months' notice contained in a notification addressed to the

---

1. Heading added according to the provisions of Protocol No. 11 (ETS No. 155).
2. Text amended according to the provisions of Protocol No. 11 (ETS No. 155).

Secretary General of the Council of Europe, who shall inform the other High Contracting Parties.

2 Such a denunciation shall not have the effect of releasing the High Contracting Party concerned from its obligations under this Convention in respect of any act which, being capable of constituting a violation of such obligations, may have been performed by it before the date at which the denunciation became effective.

3 Any High Contracting Party which shall cease to be a member of the Council of Europe shall cease to be a Party to this Convention under the same conditions.

4[1] The Convention may be denounced in accordance with the provisions of the preceding paragraphs in respect of any territory to which it has been declared to extend under the terms of Article 56.

Article 59[2] – Signature and ratification

1 This Convention shall be open to the signature of the members of the Council of Europe. It shall be ratified. Ratifications shall be deposited with the Secretary General of the Council of Europe.

2 The present Convention shall come into force after the deposit of ten instruments of ratification.

3 As regards any signatory ratifying subsequently, the Convention shall come into force at the date of the deposit of its instrument of ratification.

4 The Secretary General of the Council of Europe shall notify all the members of the Council of Europe of the entry into force of the Convention, the names of the High Contracting Parties who have ratified it, and the deposit of all instruments of ratification which may be effected subsequently.

Done at Rome this 4th day of November 1950, in English and French, both texts being equally authentic, in a single copy which shall remain deposited in the archives of the Council of Europe. The Secretary General shall transmit certified copies to each of the signatories.

---

1. Text amended according to the provisions of Protocol No. 11 (ETS No. 155).
2. Heading added according to the provisions of Protocol No. 11 (ETS No. 155).

Protocol to the Convention for the Protection of Human Rights and Fundamental Freedoms
(European Treaty Series, No. 9)

Paris, 20.III.1952

Headings of articles added and text amended according to the provisions of Protocol No. 11 (ETS No. 155) as from its entry into force on 1 November 1998.

The governments signatory hereto, being members of the Council of Europe,

Being resolved to take steps to ensure the collective enforcement of certain rights and freedoms other than those already included in Section I of the Convention for the Protection of Human Rights and Fundamental Freedoms signed at Rome on 4 November 1950 (hereinafter referred to as "the Convention"),

Have agreed as follows:

Article 1 – Protection of property

Every natural or legal person is entitled to the peaceful enjoyment of his possessions. No one shall be deprived of his possessions except in the public interest and subject to the conditions provided for by law and by the general principles of international law.

The preceding provisions shall not, however, in any way impair the right of a State to enforce such laws as it deems necessary to control the use of property in accordance with the general interest or to secure the payment of taxes or other contributions or penalties.

Article 2 – Right to education

No person shall be denied the right to education. In the exercise of any functions which it assumes in relation to education and to teaching, the State shall respect the right of parents to ensure such education and teaching in conformity with their own religious and philosophical convictions.

Article 3 – Right to free elections

The High Contracting Parties undertake to hold free elections at reasonable intervals by secret ballot, under conditions which will ensure the free expression of the opinion of the people in the choice of the legislature.

Article 4[1] – Territorial application

Any High Contracting Party may at the time of signature or ratification or at any time thereafter communicate to the Secretary General of the Council of Europe a declaration stating the extent to which it undertakes that the provisions of the present Protocol shall apply to such of the territories for the international relations of which it is responsible as are named therein.

Any High Contracting Party which has communicated a declaration in virtue of the preceding paragraph may from time to time communicate a further declaration modifying the terms of any former declaration or terminating the application of the provisions of this Protocol in respect of any territory.

A declaration made in accordance with this article shall be deemed to have been made in accordance with paragraph 1 of Article 56 of the Convention.

Article 5 – Relationship to the Convention

As between the High Contracting Parties the provisions of Articles 1, 2, 3 and 4 of this Protocol shall be regarded as additional articles to the Convention and all the provisions of the Convention shall apply accordingly.

Article 6 – Signature and ratification

This Protocol shall be open for signature by the members of the Council of Europe, who are the signatories of the Convention; it shall be ratified at the same time as or after the ratification of the Convention. It shall enter into force after the deposit of ten instruments of ratification. As regards any signatory ratifying subsequently, the Protocol shall enter into force at the date of the deposit of its instrument of ratification.

The instruments of ratification shall be deposited with the Secretary General of the Council of Europe, who will notify all members of the names of those who have ratified.

Done at Paris on the 20th day of March 1952, in English and French, both texts being equally authentic, in a single copy which shall remain deposited in the archives of the Council of Europe. The Secretary General shall transmit certified copies to each of the signatory governments.

---

1. Text amended according to the provisions of Protocol No. 11 (ETS No. 155).

Protocol No. 4 to the Convention for the Protection of Human Rights and Fundamental Freedoms securing certain rights and freedoms other than those already included in the Convention and in the first Protocol thereto
(European Treaty Series, No. 46)

Strasbourg, 16.IX.1963

Headings of articles added and text amended according to the provisions of Protocol No. 11 (ETS No. 155) as of its entry into force on 1 November 1998.

The governments signatory hereto, being members of the Council of Europe,

Being resolved to take steps to ensure the collective enforcement of certain rights and freedoms other than those already included in Section 1 of the Convention for the Protection of Human Rights and Fundamental Freedoms signed at Rome on 4th November 1950 (hereinafter referred to as the "Convention") and in Articles 1 to 3 of the First Protocol to the Convention, signed at Paris on 20th March 1952,

Have agreed as follows:

Article 1 – Prohibition of imprisonment for debt

No one shall be deprived of his liberty merely on the ground of inability to fulfil a contractual obligation.

Article 2 – Freedom of movement

1 Everyone lawfully within the territory of a State shall, within that territory, have the right to liberty of movement and freedom to choose his residence.

2 Everyone shall be free to leave any country, including his own.

3 No restrictions shall be placed on the exercise of these rights other than such as are in accordance with law and are necessary in a democratic society in the interests of national security or public safety, for the maintenance of ordre public, for the prevention of crime, for the protection of

health or morals, or for the protection of the rights and freedoms of others.

4   The rights set forth in paragraph 1 may also be subject, in particular areas, to restrictions imposed in accordance with law and justified by the public interest in a democratic society.

Article 3 – Prohibition of expulsion of nationals

1   No one shall be expelled, by means either of an individual or of a collective measure, from the territory of the State of which he is a national.

2   No one shall be deprived of the right to enter the territory of the state of which he is a national.

Article 4 – Prohibition of collective expulsion of aliens

Collective expulsion of aliens is prohibited.

Article 5 – Territorial application

1   Any High Contracting Party may, at the time of signature or ratification of this Protocol, or at any time thereafter, communicate to the Secretary General of the Council of Europe a declaration stating the extent to which it undertakes that the provisions of this Protocol shall apply to such of the territories for the international relations of which it is responsible as are named therein.

2   Any High Contracting Party which has communicated a declaration in virtue of the preceding paragraph may, from time to time, communicate a further declaration modifying the terms of any former declaration or terminating the application of the provisions of this Protocol in respect of any territory.

3[1] A declaration made in accordance with this article shall be deemed to have been made in accordance with paragraph 1 of Article 56 of the Convention.

4   The territory of any State to which this Protocol applies by virtue of ratification or acceptance by that State, and each territory to which this Protocol is applied by virtue of a declaration by that State under this article, shall be treated as separate territories for the purpose of the references in Articles 2 and 3 to the territory of a State.

5[2] Any State which has made a declaration in accordance with paragraph 1 or 2 of this Article may at any time thereafter declare on behalf of one or more of the territories to which the declaration relates that it accepts the

1. Text amended according to the provisions of Protocol No. 11 (ETS No. 155).
2. Text added according to the provisions of Protocol No. 11 (ETS No. 155).

competence of the Court to receive applications from individuals, non-governmental organisations or groups of individuals as provided in Article 34 of the Convention in respect of all or any of Articles 1 to 4 of this Protocol.

Article 6[1] – Relationship to the Convention

As between the High Contracting Parties the provisions of Articles 1 to 5 of this Protocol shall be regarded as additional Articles to the Convention, and all the provisions of the Convention shall apply accordingly.

Article 7 – Signature and ratification

1   This Protocol shall be open for signature by the members of the Council of Europe who are the signatories of the Convention; it shall be ratified at the same time as or after the ratification of the Convention. It shall enter into force after the deposit of five instruments of ratification. As regards any signatory ratifying subsequently, the Protocol shall enter into force at the date of the deposit of its instrument of ratification.

2   The instruments of ratification shall be deposited with the Secretary General of the Council of Europe, who will notify all members of the names of those who have ratified.

In witness whereof the undersigned, being duly authorised thereto, have signed this Protocol.

Done at Strasbourg, this 16th day of September 1963, in English and in French, both texts being equally authoritative, in a single copy which shall remain deposited in the archives of the Council of Europe. The Secretary General shall transmit certified copies to each of the signatory states.

---

1. Text amended according to the provisions of Protocol No. 11 (ETS No. 155).

Protocol No. 6 to the Convention for the Protection of Human Rights and Fundamental Freedoms concerning the abolition of the death penalty
(European Treaty Series, No. 114)

Strasbourg, 28.IV.1983

Headings of articles added and text amended according to the provisions of Protocol No. 11 (ETS No. 155) as of its entry into force on 1 November 1998.

The member States of the Council of Europe, signatory to this Protocol to the Convention for the Protection of Human Rights and Fundamental Freedoms, signed at Rome on 4 November 1950 (hereinafter referred to as "the Convention"),

Considering that the evolution that has occurred in several member States of the Council of Europe expresses a general tendency in favour of abolition of the death penalty;

Have agreed as follows:

Article 1 – Abolition of the death penalty

The death penalty shall be abolished. No one shall be condemned to such penalty or executed.

Article 2 – Death penalty in time of war

A State may make provision in its law for the death penalty in respect of acts committed in time of war or of imminent threat of war; such penalty shall be applied only in the instances laid down in the law and in accordance with its provisions. The State shall communicate to the Secretary General of the Council of Europe the relevant provisions of that law.

Article 3 – Prohibition of derogations

No derogation from the provisions of this Protocol shall be made under Article 15 of the Convention.

Article 4[1] – Prohibition of reservations

No reservation may be made under Article 57 of the Convention in respect of the provisions of this Protocol.

Article 5 – Territorial application

1   Any State may at the time of signature or when depositing its instrument of ratification, acceptance or approval, specify the territory or territories to which this Protocol shall apply.

2   Any State may at any later date, by a declaration addressed to the Secretary General of the Council of Europe, extend the application of this Protocol to any other territory specified in the declaration. In respect of such territory the Protocol shall enter into force on the first day of the month following the date of receipt of such declaration by the Secretary General.

3   Any declaration made under the two preceding paragraphs may, in respect of any territory specified in such declaration, be withdrawn by a notification addressed to the Secretary General. The withdrawal shall become effective on the first day of the month following the date of receipt of such notification by the Secretary General.

Article 6 – Relationship to the Convention

As between the States Parties the provisions of Articles 1 and 5 of this Protocol shall be regarded as additional articles to the Convention and all the provisions of the Convention shall apply accordingly.

Article 7 – Signature and ratification

The Protocol shall be open for signature by the member States of the Council of Europe, signatories to the Convention. It shall be subject to ratification, acceptance or approval. A member State of the Council of Europe may not ratify, accept or approve this Protocol unless it has, simultaneously or previously, ratified the Convention. Instruments of ratification, acceptance or approval shall be deposited with the Secretary General of the Council of Europe.

Article 8 – Entry into force

1   This Protocol shall enter into force on the first day of the month following the date on which five member States of the Council of Europe have expressed their consent to be bound by the Protocol in accordance with the provisions of Article 7.

---

1. Text amended according to the provisions of Protocol No. 11 (ETS No. 155).

2   In respect of any member State which subsequently expresses its consent to be bound by it, the Protocol shall enter into force on the first day of the month following the date of the deposit of the instrument of ratification, acceptance or approval.

Article 9 – Depositary functions

The Secretary General of the Council of Europe shall notify the member States of the Council of:

a   any signature;

b   the deposit of any instrument of ratification, acceptance or approval;

c   any date of entry into force of this Protocol in accordance with Articles 5 and 8;

d   any other act, notification or communication relating to this Protocol.

In witness whereof the undersigned, being duly authorised thereto, have signed this Protocol.

Done at Strasbourg, this 28th day of April 1983, in English and in French, both texts being equally authentic, in a single copy which shall be deposited in the archives of the Council of Europe. The Secretary General of the Council of Europe shall transmit certified copies to each member State of the Council of Europe.

Protocol No. 7 to the Convention for the Protection of Human Rights and Fundamental Freedoms
(European Treaty Series, No. 117)

Strasbourg, 22.XI.1984

Headings of articles added and text amended according to the provisions of Protocol No. 11 (ETS No. 155) as of its entry into force on 1 November 1998.

The member States of the Council of Europe signatory hereto,

Being resolved to take further steps to ensure the collective enforcement of certain rights and freedoms by means of the Convention for the Protection of Human Rights and Fundamental Freedoms signed at Rome on 4 November 1950 (hereinafter referred to as "the Convention"),

Have agreed as follows:

Article 1 – Procedural safeguards relating to expulsion of aliens

1   An alien lawfully resident in the territory of a State shall not be expelled therefrom except in pursuance of a decision reached in accordance with law and shall be allowed:

a   to submit reasons against his expulsion,

b   to have his case reviewed, and

c   to be represented for these purposes before the competent authority or a person or persons designated by that authority.

2   An alien may be expelled before the exercise of his rights under paragraph 1.a, b and c of this Article, when such expulsion is necessary in the interests of public order or is grounded on reasons of national security.

Article 2 – Right of appeal in criminal matters

1   Everyone convicted of a criminal offence by a tribunal shall have the right to have his conviction or sentence reviewed by a higher tribunal. The exercise of this right, including the grounds on which it may be exercised, shall be governed by law.

2   This right may be subject to exceptions in regard to offences of a minor character, as prescribed by law, or in cases in which the person concerned

was tried in the first instance by the highest tribunal or was convicted following an appeal against acquittal.

Article 3 – Compensation for wrongful conviction

When a person has by a final decision been convicted of a criminal offence and when subsequently his conviction has been reversed, or he has been pardoned, on the ground that a new or newly discovered fact shows conclusively that there has been a miscarriage of justice, the person who has suffered punishment as a result of such conviction shall be compensated according to the law or the practice of the State concerned, unless it is proved that the non-disclosure of the unknown fact in time is wholly or partly attributable to him.

Article 4 – Right not to be tried or punished twice

1   No one shall be liable to be tried or punished again in criminal proceedings under the jurisdiction of the same State for an offence for which he has already been finally acquitted or convicted in accordance with the law and penal procedure of that State.

2   The provisions of the preceding paragraph shall not prevent the reopening of the case in accordance with the law and penal procedure of the State concerned, if there is evidence of new or newly discovered facts, or if there has been a fundamental defect in the previous proceedings, which could affect the outcome of the case.

3   No derogation from this Article shall be made under Article 15 of the Convention.

Article 5 – Equality between spouses

Spouses shall enjoy equality of rights and responsibilities of a private law character between them, and in their relations with their children, as to marriage, during marriage and in the event of its dissolution. This Article shall not prevent States from taking such measures as are necessary in the interests of the children.

Article 6 – Territorial application

1   Any State may at the time of signature or when depositing its instrument of ratification, acceptance or approval, specify the territory or territories to which the Protocol shall apply and state the extent to which it undertakes that the provisions of this Protocol shall apply to such territory or territories.

2   Any State may at any later date, by a declaration addressed to the Secretary General of the Council of Europe, extend the application of this Protocol to any other territory specified in the declaration. In respect of such

territory the Protocol shall enter into force on the first day of the month following the expiration of a period of two months after the date of receipt by the Secretary General of such declaration.

3   Any declaration made under the two preceding paragraphs may, in respect of any territory specified in such declaration, be withdrawn or modified by a notification addressed to the Secretary General. The withdrawal or modification shall become effective on the first day of the month following the expiration of a period of two months after the date of receipt of such notification by the Secretary General.

4[1]   A declaration made in accordance with this Article shall be deemed to have been made in accordance with paragraph 1 of Article 56 of the Convention.

5   The territory of any State to which this Protocol applies by virtue of ratification, acceptance or approval by that State, and each territory to which this Protocol is applied by virtue of a declaration by that State under this Article, may be treated as separate territories for the purpose of the reference in Article 1 to the territory of a State.

6[2]   Any State which has made a declaration in accordance with paragraph 1 or 2 of this Article may at any time thereafter declare on behalf of one or more of the territories to which the declaration relates that it accepts the competence of the Court to receive applications from individuals, non-governmental organisations or groups of individuals as provided in Article 34 of the Convention in respect of Articles 1 to 5 of this Protocol.

Article 7[1] – Relationship to the Convention

As between the States Parties, the provisions of Article 1 to 6 of this Protocol shall be regarded as additional Articles to the Convention, and all the provisions of the Convention shall apply accordingly.

Article 8 – Signature and ratification

This Protocol shall be open for signature by member States of the Council of Europe which have signed the Convention. It is subject to ratification, acceptance or approval. A member State of the Council of Europe may not ratify, accept or approve this Protocol without previously or simultaneously ratifying the Convention. Instruments of ratification, acceptance or approval shall be deposited with the Secretary General of the Council of Europe.

---

1. Text amended according to the provisions of Protocol No. 11 (ETS No. 155).
2. Text added according to the provisions of Protocol No. 11 (ETS No. 155).

Article 9 – Entry into force

1 This Protocol shall enter into force on the first day of the month following the expiration of a period of two months after the date on which seven member States of the Council of Europe have expressed their consent to be bound by the Protocol in accordance with the provisions of Article 8.

2 In respect of any member State which subsequently expresses its consent to be bound by it, the Protocol shall enter into force on the first day of the month following the expiration of a period of two months after the date of the deposit of the instrument of ratification, acceptance or approval.

Article 10 – Depositary functions

The Secretary General of the Council of Europe shall notify all the member States of the Council of Europe of:

a any signature;

b the deposit of any instrument of ratification, acceptance or approval;

c any date of entry into force of this Protocol in accordance with Articles 6 and 9;

d any other act, notification or declaration relating to this Protocol.

In witness whereof the undersigned, being duly authorised thereto, have signed this Protocol.

Done at Strasbourg, this 22nd day of November 1984, in English and French, both texts being equally authentic, in a single copy which shall be deposited in the archives of the Council of Europe. The Secretary General of the Council of Europe shall transmit certified copies to each member State of the Council of Europe.

Explanatory report to Protocol No. 11 to the European Convention on Human Rights[1]

I Introduction

1   In November 1991, the Ministers of Foreign Affairs, meeting at the 89th session of the Committee of Ministers of the Council of Europe, instructed their Deputies to give absolute priority to speeding up work on the reform of the control mechanism of the European Convention on Human Rights.

2   At their 91st session in November 1992, the Ministers noted that the technical background work on this subject had been completed and that various proposals awaited consideration as to the substance of the reform (notably the creation of a single Court or the introduction of a two-tier judicial system).[2] The Ministers reiterated the importance they attached to this urgent problem and, having also noted Recommendation 1194 (1992) of the Parliamentary Assembly – which supported the proposal to create a single Court as a full-time body in replacement of the existing European Commission and Court of Human Rights – agreed that a search for a rapid solution should feature prominently among the Organisation's priorities.

3   At the 92nd session of the Committee of Ministers, held in May 1993, the Ministers noted that there had been significant progress at the level of their Deputies in recent weeks on the preparation of a mandate, and instructed their Deputies "to complete this work urgently in time for the meeting of the Steering Committee for Human Rights (CDDH) starting on 7 June 1993, with a view to preparing a draft protocol to amend the European Convention on Human Rights for submission to Heads of State and Government in Vienna in October 1993".

4   On 28 May 1993, during a special meeting, the Ministers' Deputies adopted a decision assigning *ad hoc* terms of reference to the CDDH. The text of the terms of reference were:

"The Committee of Ministers stresses the necessity of a reform of the supervisory mechanism of the Convention for the Protection of Human Rights and Fundamental Freedoms, with the aim of improving efficiency and shortening the time taken for individual applications, at minimum cost.

---

1. Unless otherwise stated, article references are to the articles of the Convention as amended by this Protocol.
2. For further details consult the Council of Europe document entitled "Reform of the control system of the European Convention on Human Rights", doc. H (92) 14 (also published in Vol. 14 *Human Rights Law Journal* (H.R.L.J.), 1993, pp. 31-48).

For this reason the Committee of Ministers instructs the CDDH to prepare a draft amending protocol to the Convention, restructuring the existing supervisory mechanism by replacing it with:

a a Court which:

- should consist of a number of judges equal to that of the members of the Council of Europe;
- should work in committees and Chambers; and
- must be provided with:
  - an effective mechanism for the filtering of applications;
  - an effective procedure to enable friendly settlements;
  - an appropriate structure to ensure the quality and consistency of its case-law and to enable a re-hearing in exceptional cases, for example those raising serious questions affecting the interpretation or application of the Convention; provision should be made for the presence of a national judge in any such re-hearing;

b the Committee of Ministers retaining its competence under Article 54, it being understood that its competence to deal with individual applications under the present Article 32 of the Convention is abolished.

The CDDH should also examine:

- whether the right of individual petition should remain optional or not;
- the way in which inter-State applications should be dealt with;
- the role and functions of possible Advocates-General."

Furthermore, the terms of reference of the CDDH stipulated that the mandate be completed by "30 September 1993, with a view to submitting the draft Protocol to amend the European Convention on Human Rights to Heads of State and Government in Vienna on 8-9 October 1993".

5 In June 1993, the CDDH requested the Committee of Experts for the Improvement of Procedures for the Protection of Human Rights (DH-PR), a subordinate body of the CDDH, to prepare, as a matter of utmost priority, a draft protocol in accordance with the terms of reference assigned to it by the Ministers' Deputies. At the Vienna Summit, held on 8-9 October 1993, the Heads of State and Government of the Council of Europe member States mandated the Committee of Ministers to finalise the draft protocol with a view to adopting a text and opening it for signature at its ministerial meeting in May 1994. The draft protocol prepared by the DH-PR and subsequently finalised by the CDDH – after due consultation of the European Commission and Court of Human Rights as well as the Parliamentary Assembly – was submitted to the Committee of Ministers, which adopted the text at the 511bis meeting of the Ministers' Deputies held on 20 April 1994. The text was opened for signature by member States of the Council of Europe signatories to the European Convention on 11 May 1994.

II Background

6   The idea of a European Convention on Human Rights to be implemented by a Court to which individuals would have access can be traced back to the Congress of Europe, convened by the International Committee of Movements for European Unity and held at The Hague from 8 to 10 May 1948. In their "Message to Europeans" adopted at the final plenary session, the Congress delegates pledged *inter alia*:

"2   We desire a Charter of Human Rights guaranteeing liberty of thought, assembly and expression as well as the right to form a political opposition;

3   We desire a Court of Justice with adequate sanctions for the implementation of this Charter;".

The resolution adopted by the Congress on the proposal of its Political Committee should also be noted:

"The Congress –

6   Is convinced that in the interest of human values and human liberty, the [proposed] Assembly should make proposals for the establishment of a Court of Justice with adequate sanctions for the implementation of this Charter [of Human Rights], and to this end any citizen of the associated countries shall have redress before the Court, at any time and with the least possible delay, of any violation of his rights as formulated in the Charter."

7   The idea of a Human Rights Charter and a Court of Justice was subsequently examined in depth by the European Movement, which on 12 July 1949 submitted the text of a draft European Convention on Human Rights to the Committee of Ministers. This text notably made provision not only for a Court but also for a Human Rights Commission, to which litigants would first have to submit their case. It was foreseen that this body would be empowered to reject without investigation petitions from individuals who had failed to exhaust domestic remedies and that, moreover, its authorisation would be required for an individual to initiate proceedings before the Court.

The proposal for a Human Rights Commission, in addition to a Court, was made to counter the criticism that the latter would be inundated with frivolous litigation and its facilities exploited for political ends. The subsequent debates in the Consultative (now renamed "Parliamentary") Assembly and the bodies established by the Committee of Ministers to draw up the Convention confirmed that these fears were deeply felt.

8   The creation of a European Commission of Human Rights was in fact not a contentious issue during the drafting of the Convention. On the other hand, there was considerable opposition to the creation of a Court, it being argued that it would not correspond to a real need of the member States. Articles 46 and 48 of the Convention represented a compromise between this position and that of those States which felt the creation of a Court was

essential (the controversy over whether individuals should have the right to address petitions to the Commission was, of course, settled in a similar way).

9 The net result was the tripartite structure, which entered into force on 3 September 1953:[1] the Commission – to consider the admissibility of petitions, to establish the facts, to promote friendly settlements and, if appropriate, to give an opinion as to whether or not the petitions reveal a violation of the Convention; the Court – to give a final and binding judgment on cases referred to it by the Commission or by a Contracting Party concerned;[2] the Committee of Ministers – to give a final and binding decision on cases which cannot be referred to the Court or which, for one reason or another, are not referred to it.

The idea of creating a single Court ("merger" of the Commission and the Court)

10 The possibility of "merging" the Commission and Court into a single body was apparently first evoked at the 8th meeting (July 1982) of the Committee of Experts for the Improvement of the Procedure under the European Convention on Human Rights (DH-PR)[3] during an exchange of views with representatives of the Commission, and since that time it has featured on the DH-PR Committee's list of possible long-term reforms. However, it was not until the European Ministerial Conference on Human Rights (Vienna, March 1985) that the "merger" idea was raised for the first time at a political level.

11 The possibility of a "merger" i.e., the creation of a single Court, was in fact broached in the report on the "functioning of the organs of the European Convention on Human Rights" presented by the Swiss delegation at the above-mentioned Conference (see doc. MDH (85) 1), and was referred to – with varying degrees of support or opposition – in a number of other contributions.

In Conference Resolution No. 1, the Ministers, after referring to "the need to examine the possibility of introducing further improvements (to the Convention's system of control), including as appropriate measures of a more far-reaching nature", underlined that the body of experts entrusted with the task of examining such possible further improvements "should bear in mind the Swiss delegation's report as well as the observations made by other delegations".

12 The Ministerial Conference also stimulated discussion of the "merger" idea (creation of a single Court) in other fora. It was raised, for example,

---

1. See *European Convention on Human Rights* (1994), *passim*.
2. It was not considered appropriate for the individual applicant himself to be allowed to refer the case to the Court (see further the Collected Edition of the *Travaux Préparatoires* of the Convention, Volume IV, page 44). Cf Protocol No. 9 to the Convention.
3. The DH-PR Committee is now called "Committee of Experts for the Improvement of Procedure for the Protection of Human Rights" (see para. 5 above).

during the debates at the 6th International Colloquy about the European Convention on Human Rights held at Seville in November 1985. Again, the "merger of the European Commission and European Court of Human Rights" was the subject of a two-day colloquy held at the University of Neuchâtel in March 1986, at which participated politicians, members of the Convention's organs, government officials, practising lawyers and other persons concerned by or interested in the envisaged reform.[1]

13 Thereupon, the DH-PR – upon the instructions of the CDDH – examined the idea of "merger" between December 1985 and December 1987, and prepared a report on this subject for the CDDH.

In January 1989, the Committee of Ministers decided – upon the request of the CDDH – to declassify the report of the DH-PR, in order to facilitate the examination of the "merger" idea within interested circles (published as doc. H (89) 2).[2]

14 Both within the CDDH and the DH-PR opinions remained divided on the advisability of the proposed reform. There was, however, general agreement within the CDDH that consideration of the reform should be pursued and the CDDH thereupon instructed the DH-PR to draw up the detailed structure of a possible single Court system, to examine methods of implementation and, at a suitable moment, to seek information on the budgetary implications of the proposal. At its 28th meeting, in June 1990, the CDDH examined the DH-PR's "detailed structure of a possible single Court system".[3] Discussion on this subject was then postponed with the request that the DH-PR not pursue consideration of methods of implementation and the question of budgetary implications.

The Dutch-Swedish initiative

15 In the meantime, initiatives had been undertaken by the Dutch and Swedish authorities to try to get out of the existing impasse. The proposals, put forward almost simultaneously by the Netherlands and Sweden in October 1990, turned out to be very similar.

16 The central idea in both proposals was that the opinions of the Commission under Article 31 of the Convention – in so far as individual applications were concerned – would have been transformed into legally binding decisions. In other words, there would have been established a two-tier judicial system, i.e. the Commission operating like a court of first instance from which individual applicants and States would be accorded the right to appeal to the Court against the Commission's decision on the merits, subject to leave

---

1. See "Merger of the European Commission and European Court of Human Rights", in Vol. 8 H.R.L.J., 1987, pp. 1-244, for the colloquy's proceedings. See also Recommendation 1087 (1988) of the Parliamentary Assembly, adopted on 7 October 1988.
2. Also published in Vol. 14 H.R.L.J., see footnote 1, p. 41.
3. See doc. H (93) 14, pp. 20-27 (also published in Vol. 14 H.R.L.J., see footnote 1, p. 41).

to appeal being granted by the Court. These proposals envisaged no changes in the present procedures relating to inter-State cases, and would have – as Protocol No. 9 to the Convention has partially done – placed individual applicants and States on an equal footing to bring cases before the Court. In addition, the proposals entailed the abandonment of the role played by the Committee of Ministers under Article 32 of the Convention in respect of individual applications.

17 These proposals were examined in depth by the DH-PR, which submitted its report on the matter to the CDDH in March 1992.[1] Although a majority of the experts in the DH-PR and CDDH was in favour of an eventual two-tier system as proposed by the Netherlands and Sweden, no consensus as to such a reform could be reached.

18 Having tried unsuccessfully to reach agreement on the proposals for a reform, the CDDH, in October 1992, referred the different proposals to the Committee of Ministers in order to obtain a clear mandate for its further work on reform. On 28 May 1993 the Committee of Ministers adopted the decision assigning the *ad hoc* terms of reference to the CDDH as mentioned in paragraph 4 above. This decision was endorsed by the Council of Europe's Heads of State and Government at the Vienna Summit in the "Vienna Declaration" of 9 October 1993.

III The urgent need to restructure the control machinery established by the Convention

19 Although the question of a reform of the supervisory machinery has been discussed since the beginning of the 1980s, the need for a reform is considered increasingly urgent as a growing number of complaints has been lodged with the Commission; in addition, new States have joined the system. The increasing workload of the Commission has also resulted in more cases being referred to the Court in the last few years.

20 The number of applications registered with the Commission has increased from 404 in 1981 to 2037 in 1993. This figure can be expected to increase significantly in view of the fact that the system has become better known to individuals in member States, and in view of the fact that new States have and will become Parties to the Convention. By the year 2000, there may well be 35-40 States Parties to the Convention. The number of judges and members of the Commission will increase in a corresponding manner.

21 The backlog of cases before the Commission is considerable. At the end of the Commission's session in January 1994, the number of pending cases stood at 2672, more than 1 487 of which had not yet been looked at by the

1. For a detailed description of the Dutch and Swedish proposals, see note 1, p. 41, at pp. 28-40 (as to the views of the members of the Court and the Commission, see pp. 41-48).

Commission. It takes on average over 5 years for a case to be finally determined by the Court or the Committee of Ministers.

Also, whereas up to 1988 there were never more than 25 cases referred to the Court in one year, 31 were referred in 1989, 61 in 1990, 93 in 1991, 50 in 1992 and 52 in 1993, and it is probable that the number will increase even more in the next few years when the full effects will be felt of Protocol No. 8 regarding the Commission. Likewise at the end of 1992 the Committee of Ministers had before it 15 cases for examination under Article 32 of the Convention; the figure was 189 at the end of 1993.

22 In the light of these facts, the Committee of Ministers has, on several occasions, stressed the urgency of reform, most recently at its 92nd session on 14 May 1993. The Parliamentary Assembly has also addressed this question. In its Recommendation 1194 (1992), adopted on 6 October 1992, the Parliamentary Assembly

"[noted] that the number of Council of Europe member states has risen [...] and will continue to rise in the next few years and that the considerable increase in the number of applications submitted to the Commission and to the Court is thus to be expected.

[It expected] that the number of individual applications will increase disproportionately to the population of the new member states as, contrary to older member states, the Council of Europe's system for the protection of human rights constitutes for them an important element for the building-up of fundamental rights, democracy and the rule of law.

[Maintaining] that the real test for its system of the protection of human rights is still to come and that the reform of the control mechanism of the Convention is therefore of the utmost importance for the Council of Europe."

It then recommended that the Committee of Ministers

"i take the necessary steps to reform the control mechanism of the European Convention on Human Rights without delay;

ii in doing so, give clear preference to the proposal to create a single court as a full-time body in place of the existing Commission and Court;

iii refrain from opting for a temporary solution that would further delay the necessary reform."

23 The reform proposed is thus principally aimed at restructuring the system, so as to shorten the length of Strasbourg proceedings. There is need for a supervising machinery that can work efficiently and at acceptable costs even with forty member States and which can maintain the authority and quality of the case-law in the future.

This point was emphasised by the Council of Europe's Heads of State and Government in the "Vienna Declaration" of 9 October 1993

"Since the Convention entered into force in 1953 the number of contracting States has almost tripled and more countries will accede after becoming members of the Council of Europe. We are of the opinion that it has become urgently necessary to adapt the present control mechanism to this development in order to be able to maintain in the future effective international protection for human rights. The purpose of this reform is to enhance the efficiency of the means of protection, to shorten procedures and to maintain the present high quality of human rights protection."

24 The creation of a single Court is intended to prevent the overlapping of a certain amount of work and also to avoid certain delays which are inherent in the present system.

25 Finally, this Protocol aims at strengthening the judicial elements of the system.

IV Main features of the single Court system

26 The new single Court will replace two of the existing supervisory organs created by the European Convention on Human Rights and will perform the functions carried out by these organs. The Committee of Ministers will retain its competence under former Article 54; its competence under former Article 32 of the Convention will be abolished.

Competence of the new Court

27 The Court will have jurisdiction in all matters concerning the interpretation and application of the Convention including inter-State cases as well as individual applications. In addition, the Court will, as at present, be able to give advisory opinions when so requested by the Committee of Ministers.

28 The Court will function on a permanent basis.

Composition of the Court

29 The Court will consist of a number of judges equal to that of the State Parties to the Convention, elected, as at present, by the Parliamentary Assembly with respect to each State Party. The members of the Court will be elected for a period of six years; they can be re-elected.

30 The Court will have a registry.

31 Judges may be assisted by legal secretaries (law clerks), i.e. assistants appointed for a specific period of time to work on case-files.

Organisation of the Court

32 When deciding cases the Court will sit in committees, Chambers and in a Grand Chamber. The judge elected in respect of the State concerned will always sit in the Chambers and Grand Chamber. Organisational matters will be dealt with by the Court in plenary, comprising all judges.

33 Committees will consist of three judges, Chambers of seven judges and the Grand Chamber of seventeen judges. There will be no quorum. The Court will appoint substitute members so that committees and Chambers can sit with the required composition of judges.

34 Committees will be set up by Chambers for a fixed period of time. Chambers will themselves determine the judges and substitute judges who are to sit in the committees. Committees will only have the power to declare cases inadmissible or strike them from the list.

35 Chambers will also be set up by the Court for a fixed period of time. The Court will designate the seven judges who will sit in a Chamber. The Court will appoint the judges and substitute judges in a way which may be specified in its rules. The possibility that a judge may be a member of two Chambers is not excluded.

36 There will be a Grand Chamber of seventeen judges to decide on individual as well as inter-State applications referred to it and to consider requests for advisory opinions. The President of the Court, the Vice-Presidents, the Presidents of the Chambers and the judge elected in respect of the State against which the application is lodged, will be *ex officio* members of the Grand Chamber. The other judges will be appointed by the Court in a way specified in the rules. When the Grand Chamber examines cases referred to it under Article 43, of the Chamber concerned only the judge elected in respect of the State and the President of the Chamber which rendered the judgment may sit in the Grand Chamber.

37 The Court may determine in its rules that members of the Grand Chamber, other than the *ex officio* members, be drawn by lot for every case.

The Court may also set up a Grand Chamber for a fixed period. Judges precluded from taking part in certain cases by virtue of Article 27, paragraph 3, will then have to be replaced by other judges, e.g., substitute members or judges chosen by lot.

Procedure before the Court

38 The Court will receive applications from:

a   any person, non-governmental organisation or group of individuals claiming to be the victim of a violation of the Convention by one of the States Parties; or

b   a State Party in the case of inter-State applications.

39 As the Secretariat of the Commission does at present, the registry of the new Court will communicate with applicants in order to deal with any matters requiring clarification before registration of an application.

40 As soon as an application is registered, a judge rapporteur will be designated by a Chamber. The individual application will normally be examined by a committee, including the judge rapporteur. The committee will have the power, exercisable by unanimous vote, to declare an application inadmissible or strike it from its list of cases if such a decision can be taken without further examination. If an application is not considered inadmissible by the committee, the case will be transferred to a Chamber, which will examine both the admissibility as well as the merits of the case. Details concerning the procedure may be dealt with in the rules of the Court. The rules of the Court may provide for the immediate transfer of applications to the Chamber, when appropriate.

41 The admissibility criteria remain unchanged. Thus the intention is that the Court will continue to exercise an effective filter function, as presently performed by the Commission.

42 Subject to powers specifically attributed to committees and the Grand Chamber, Chambers will have inherent competence to examine the admissibility and the merits of all individual and inter-State applications (for inter-State cases see also paragraph 54 below).

43 As already indicated, every application registered will be allocated to a judge rapporteur. With the help of the registry of the Court, the judge rapporteur will, under the authority of the Court, prepare the case, communicate as appropriate with the parties for that purpose and may, after the case has been declared admissible, take steps with a view to a friendly settlement.

44 The procedure will be written and oral, unless otherwise decided by the Court after consultation with the parties. Subject to powers delegated to committees, the admissibility of applications will be examined by the Chambers or the Grand Chamber. The Chambers' decisions on admissibility will, in principle, be taken separately from the merits.

The facts will be established by the Court, with the co-operation of the parties. The Court will be at the disposal of the parties in order to secure a friendly settlement on the basis of respect for human rights.

45 The merits of an application will be examined by a Chamber and, exceptionally, by the Grand Chamber. The parties will present their submissions by means of a written procedure. Oral procedure will consist of a hearing at which the applicant, or a State Party in an inter-State case, and the respondent State will have the right to speak.

46 In cases with specified serious implications, a Chamber will be able to relinquish jurisdiction *proprio motu* in favour of the Grand Chamber at any

time, as long as it has not yet rendered judgment, unless one of the parties to the case objects. Such relinquishment should also speed up proceedings. Once a judgment has been rendered by a Chamber, only the parties may request that the case be referred to the Grand Chamber for a re-hearing.

47 Following the judgment delivered by a Chamber of the Court, the Grand Chamber, at the request of one of the parties to the case and in exceptional cases, will be competent to re-examine a case if the case raises serious questions concerning the interpretation or application of the Convention or its protocols, or if the cases raises an issue of general importance. The purpose is to ensure the quality and consistency of the Court's case-law by allowing for a re-examination of the most important cases if the above-mentioned conditions are met. A panel of five judges of the Grand Chamber will decide on whether a case is to be accepted for re-examination.

48 The provisions of the Protocol also provide for the participation of third parties in proceedings before the Court. In cases declared admissible, States whose nationals have lodged applications against other States Parties to the Convention, will have the possibility to submit written comments and take part in hearings.

Likewise, the President of the Court will be able to invite or authorise any Contracting State which is not Party to proceedings and any person establishing an interest in the result of any case brought before it to submit observations.

49 The Court will determine the question of just satisfaction, including that of costs and expenses.

50 The judgment of the Grand Chamber will be final. The judgment of the Chamber will become final in accordance with the new Article 44, paragraph 2, if the case in which it has been rendered is not brought before the Grand Chamber. Final judgments of the Court will be binding. The Committee of Ministers will, as at present, supervise their execution.

Procedure governing friendly settlements

51 A case may be terminated by a friendly settlement between the parties at any stage of the proceedings before the Court.

As already indicated, the Court, with the help of its registry, may assist the parties (see also paragraphs 93 and 94 below).

Outline of the procedure

52 The basic order of procedure in a case which proceeds to judgment on the merits will be, in most cases, as follows:

– lodging of application;
– preliminary contacts with the Court's registry;

- registration of application;
- assignment of application to a Chamber;
- appointment of judge rapporteur by the Chamber;
- examination by a three-member committee;
- communication of the application to the Government;
- filing of observations and establishment of facts;
- oral hearing;
- admissibility decision by Chamber;
- possibility of friendly settlement negotiations;
- judgment by the Chamber.

53 In exceptional cases an application may be referred to the Grand Chamber which will render judgment after written and, if the Court so decides, oral proceedings.

Procedure applicable to inter-State applications

54 Any State Party will be able to refer to the Court any alleged breach of the provision of the Convention by another State Party; a Chamber will have jurisdiction.

V The choice of an amending rather than an optional protocol

55 The fundamental character of the reform of the control mechanism necessitates approval by all States Parties to the Convention. Therefore, Protocol No. 11 is conceived in the form of an amending protocol, in respect of which all States Parties must express their consent to be bound in order for it to enter into force.

56 Only an amending protocol can prevent two different mechanisms of control from existing side by side. Such a parallelism would not be desirable because a homogeneous and clearly consistent development of case-law constitutes an important basis of human rights protection under the Convention. Furthermore, the existence of two groups of States subject to two different supervisory mechanisms would invariably cause considerable procedural complications, e.g. for the registry and for judges sitting in both the old and the new Courts. This would run counter to the aim of the reform to increase efficiency. Finally, the parallelism of two mechanisms of supervision could cause confusion for individual applicants, a result contrary to the aim of creating a more transparent system.

Moreover, it should be pointed out that during the Vienna Summit, the Heads of State and Government affirmed that this Protocol be submitted for ratification at the earliest possible date (see also paragraphs 5 and 23 above).

VI Commentary on the provisions of Protocol No. 11[1]

Article 1 of the amending Protocol

Article 19 – Establishment of the Court

57 The text of Article 19 follows closely that of former Article 19 of the Convention. However, unlike former Article 19 of the Convention, this and certain later articles in the text mention the protocols to the Convention; this addition reflects developments after the adoption of the Convention in 1950. Obviously, States will be bound only by the protocols they have ratified.

58 The same title as that of the former Court has been retained for the supervisory institution. This, however, should not disguise the fact that it is a new institution. The new Court is to be a permanent Court, whose seat is in Strasbourg.

Article 20 – Number of judges

59 Article 20 is based on former Article 38 of the Convention, except that the second sentence of former Article 38 of the Convention has been deleted. i.e., the condition that no two judges may be nationals of the same State has been removed. In principle, there should be no more than two judges of the same nationality on the Court. A State Party will have the possibility to put forward the name of a judge who is a national of another State Party rather than propose a judge from a State which has not ratified the Convention.

The Court consists of the number of judges equal to that of Contracting Parties rather than, as beforehand, that of the members of the Council of Europe. In this respect it was considered preferable to follow the procedure relating to the appointment of members of the Commission (see Article 20 of the former text of the Convention).

Article 21 – Criteria for office

60 Paragraphs 1 and 2 of Article 21 follow closely paragraph 3 of former Article 39 and paragraph 7 of former Article 40 of the Convention. The provision in paragraph 3 concerns incompatibility "with the demands" of this office and means that judges must be able fully to assume all the duties inherent in membership of the new permanent Court; this is an indispensable requirement for the efficient working of the Court. During their term of office judges may not engage in any activity incompatible with the full-time character of their office.

---

1. Unless otherwise stated, references to articles are to the articles of the Convention as amended by this protocol.

Article 22 – Election of judges

61 The text of Article 22 is virtually identical to that of former Article 39, paragraphs 1 and 2 of the Convention. As to paragraph 3 of former Article 39, this has been included in Article 21. The judges of the new permanent Court will be elected in respect of each State Party in the same manner as those of the Court, prior to the Convention's amendment by this Protocol, namely by the Parliamentary Assembly.

Article 23 – Terms of office

62 The text of Article 23 is similar to that of paragraphs 1 to 6 of former Article 40 of the Convention (as to paragraph 7 of that Article, see Article 21). Judges will be elected for a period of six years, as compared to nine years, as was previously the case (see Article 22, paragraph 1, of the former text of the Convention). Consequently, the rotation provisions have been amended accordingly.

If the number of judges is uneven, paragraphs 1 and 3 are to be interpreted to mean one half of the judges, minus one person.

63 Paragraph 6 adds the requirement that judges must retire at the age of 70; the Court's rules will determine in which circumstances a judge can continue to deal with a case upon reaching the age of 70, as envisaged in paragraph 7. Since the Court will function on a permanent basis, it was deemed appropriate to introduce an age limit, as exists in most domestic legal systems.

Article 24 – Dismissal

64 This Article is modelled on Article 18, paragraph 1, of the Statute of the International Court of Justice. However, unlike the latter text, which requires unanimity, in the present text dismissal from office requires a majority of two-thirds of all the judges of the Court. This provision was added in order to ensure the independence of the Court.

Article 25 – Registry and legal secretaries

65 The text of Article 25, first sentence, is derived from Rules 11 and 12 of the former Rules of Court.

66 A Registrar and one or more Deputy Registrars are elected by the Court. The Court's registry is provided by the Secretary General of the Council of Europe.

67 The second sentence is a new provision inserted into the text of the Convention in order to ensure that members of the Court can, if they so wish, be assisted by legal secretaries (law clerks). Such assistants, who may be appointed upon the proposal of the judges, must have the required qualifi-

cations and practical experience to carry out the duties assigned to them by the judges.

Article 26 – Plenary Court

68 The text of Article 26 is a substantially expanded version of former Article 41 of the Convention (see also paragraphs 32 to 37).

69 Article 26 d is modelled on former Article 55 of the Convention. In relation to the advisory jurisdiction of the Court under Articles 47 to 49, it fulfils the same function as Article 4 of the former Protocol No. 2.

70 The rules of Court will have to be adapted to the new structure and, in particular, to be supplemented on the following points: the role of the registry; the functions of the plenary Court; the constitution and the composition of the Grand Chamber, Chambers and committees; procedure on questions of admissibility and procedure concerning friendly settlement negotiations. The Rules of Procedure of the Commission will be of assistance in this connection.

71 Another matter for the rules of the new Court will be the question of publicity. The Court's proceedings (unlike those of the Commission; see former Article 33 of the Convention) will, save in exceptional circumstances, be public (see Article 40). Material relating to the friendly settlement negotiations will remain confidential (see Article 38, paragraph 2; see also Article 40, paragraph 2).

Article 27 – Committees, Chambers and Grand Chamber

72 The organisation of the Court is described above (see paragraphs 32 to 37). Cases are to be decided by committees, Chambers and the Grand Chamber. The judge elected in respect of the State concerned will sit ex officio in Chamber and in the Grand Chamber; this judge does not necessarily sit in a committee. Persons sitting in the capacity of judges, in accordance with paragraph 2, must fulfil the requirements laid down in Article 21 (with the exception of the requirement relating to the demands of a full-time office).

73 There are, as ex officio members of the Grand Chamber, the President of the Court, the Vice-Presidents, the Chamber Presidents and the judge elected in respect of the State concerned. The other judges are chosen in accordance with the Rules of the Court (Article 27, paragraph 3). To make sure that the Grand Chamber looks into the matter afresh when examining a case referred to it under Article 43, judges from the Chamber which made the initial judgment are excluded, with the exception of the President of the Chamber and the judge who sat in respect of the State concerned.

74 In order to ensure the consistency of the Court's case-law it was considered necessary to ensure that Presidents of all Chambers sit in the Grand Chamber.

The presence of the judge elected in respect of the State concerned is necessary in order to avoid *ad hoc* "national judges" in cases before the Grand Chamber.

Article 28 – Declarations of inadmissibility by committees

75 In this and other Articles, complaints submitted by persons, non-governmental organisations or groups of individuals are referred to as "applications" rather than "petitions" as in the English text of former Article 25 of the Convention. This reflects practice that existed under the former supervisory system.

76 The procedure before a committee will be similar to the procedure followed by committees that were set up within the European Commission of Human Rights. Every application will first be dealt with by the registry, which will have to perform the functions mentioned in paragraphs 39 and 52. Before registration of an application, the file of the case is to be treated as a "provisional file". After registration the case will be allocated to a judge rapporteur who will, in conformity with the Court's rules of procedure, direct the further preparation of the case. Since the Court is to function on a permanent basis, and the members of the Court will be present in Strasbourg, the judges may also be provided with the task of supervising the preparation of cases which are not registered, and in particular to keep themselves informed of their number and the length of time such cases have been pending without formal registration. This will concern, in the first place, the judge who is elected in respect of the country concerned by the application, and probably also the President of the Chamber in which this judge sits. The rules of procedure of the Court will need to specify this function in more detail.

Article 29 – Decisions by Chambers on admissibility and merits

77 The text of Article 29 clarifies that the Chamber has to examine the admissibility and the merits of the case. It can declare an application as inadmissible at any stage of the proceedings (Article 35, paragraph 4) even though it originally declared it admissible. The decision on admissibility should be reached at the earliest appropriate stage.

78 The decision on admissibility will be taken separately. It has to be reasoned (Article 45, paragraph 1). The Chamber may provide the parties with an indication of its provisional opinion on the merits. The separate decision on admissibility is important for the parties when considering whether they should start friendly settlement negotiations.

There may, however, be situations in which the Court, in exceptional cases, might not take a separate admissibility decision. This could occur, for example, where a State does not object that a case be declared admissible.

Article 30 – Relinquishment of jurisdiction to the Grand Chamber

79 The text of Article 30 is derived from Rule 51 of the former Rules of Court. Contrary to Rule 51, paragraph 1, second sentence, of the former Rules of the Court,

Article 30 does not oblige a Chamber to relinquish jurisdiction.

The reason for making relinquishment subject to the approval of the parties should be seen in the light of the introduction of the concept of "re-hearing", in accordance with the decision of the Committee of Ministers on 28 May 1993 (see paragraph 4 above). The provision is designed so as to secure the possibility that such a "re-hearing" not be adversely affected. This procedure of relinquishment, the use of which can be made any time prior to judgment, must thus be distinguished from that of a re-hearing as provided for in Article 43.

Article 31 – Powers of the Grand Chamber

80 Notwithstanding new Article 26, the Grand Chamber, as described above (see paragraphs 36, 37 and 44 to 50), replaces the plenary Court of the former system. In a Court with more than 30 judges, a plenary with all the judges could work only with difficulty. The Grand Chamber with seventeen judges will be sufficiently representative of the Court. It shall, as far as possible, provide a balanced representation of judges from each Chamber as well as a diversity of legal systems.

The plenary comprising all judges will only deal with matters of organisation mentioned in Article 26.

81 The Grand Chamber is to have competence both with regard to inter-State applications referred to it under Article 30 or 43 as well as individual applications when they are referred to it under Article 30 or 43. The Grand Chamber is also to consider requests for advisory opinions, a function which the plenary Court carried out under the former system. (See Article 3, paragraph 1, of former Protocol No. 2).

Article 32 – Jurisdiction of the Court

82 The first paragraph of Article 32 follows closely former Article 45 of the Convention, with an additional reference to its competence to consider requests for advisory opinions; the second paragraph is identical to former Article 49 of the Convention.

Article 33 – Inter-State cases

83 The text of Article 33 is based on that of former Article 24 of the Convention.

This article on inter-State cases reflects the former system whereby proceedings could be instituted before the Commission by one or more States against another State that had ratified the Convention, without the necessity for any additional acceptance of competence on the latter's part. States are, of course, bound only by the protocols they have ratified.

84 "High Contracting Party" in this Article is any State which is a Party to the Convention, as amended by this Protocol.

Article 34 – Individual applications

85 The text of Article 34 is based on that of former Article 25 of the Convention. Under the former system, cases originating in applications by private individuals or non-governmental organisations could only come into being if the State concerned had declared that it accepted the Commission's competence in the matter and could only be decided by the Court if the State had, in addition, declared that it recognised the Court's jurisdiction. It should be noted that all Contracting Parties have accepted the right of individual petition, and that full acceptance of the supervisory mechanism established by the Convention has become, *de facto*, a condition for admission to the Organisation. This has resulted in the jurisdiction of the Court, as provided in Article 34, becoming mandatory.

86 Under the former system, a case which was capable of being the subject of judicial decision (because the Court's jurisdiction was recognised) need not necessarily have been so decided because it was not referred to the Court either by the Commission or the State concerned and so was left to be determined by the Committee of Ministers. Such a situation, which was linked to the fact that the individual applicant had no power to refer his own case to the Court, was changed by Protocol No. 9. Under the new system applicants can bring their cases directly before the Court without restrictions. The present text entails the abandonment of the role played by the Committee of Ministers under former Article 32 of the Convention.

States are, of course, bound only by the protocols they have ratified. (But see also new Article 56 and paragraph 113 below.)

Article 35 – Admissibility criteria

87 Paragraph 1 of Article 35 is derived from former Article 26 of the Convention and paragraphs 2 to 4 from former Article 27. The intention here is to continue practice based on the former Commission's Rules of Procedure.

Grounds of inadmissibility, as they existed under the former system, have been left unchanged in order to provide the new Court with an effective filter mechanism. An application which is patently inadmissible can be so declared at the initial stage of the proceedings by a committee, as provided for in Article 28. The decision declaring an application inadmissible will be final. The decision on admissibility will, in most cases, be taken separately (see Article 29, second sentence).

88 Paragraph 4 of Article 35 does not signify that a State is able to raise an admissibility question at any stage of the proceedings, if it could have been raised earlier.

It is nevertheless important to stress that the Court will be able to reject an application at any stage of the proceedings – even without an oral hearing – if it finds the existence of one of the grounds of non-acceptance provided in Article 35 (cf Article 29 of the Convention's former text).

89 Copies of all decisions declaring applications inadmissible should be transmitted to the States concerned for information.

Article 36 – Third-party intervention

90 This article provides for the possibility for States Parties and other interested persons to take part in proceedings before the Court.

Paragraph 1 gives a State Party one of whose nationals is an applicant the right to submit written comments and to make an oral intervention once the case has come before a Chamber or the Grand Chamber (cf Article 48.b of the former text of the Convention).

91 Paragraph 2 follows closely Rule 37, paragraph 2, of the former Rules of Court. The person concerned may be a natural or a legal person.

States and persons taking part in such proceedings are not parties to the proceedings.

Article 37 – Striking out applications

92 The text of Article 37 follows closely that of former Article 30, paragraphs 1 and 3, of the Convention. As was the case under former Article 30 of the Convention, the power to strike out is extended to applications submitted by a State under Article 33 as well as applications submitted by an individual under Article 34. Although it could be argued that an inherent power to strike out cases is vested in any court, this Article has been included to avoid any doubts on the matter.

Article 38 – Examination of the case and friendly settlement proceedings

93 The text of Article 38, paragraph 1, is based on that of former Article 28, paragraph 1, of the Convention, although paragraph 1 a. of the latter has

been somewhat shortened. The Court is responsible for the establishment of the facts and may conduct an investigation on the understanding that the parties furnish the Court with all the relevant information. Parties to friendly settlement proceedings will not be at liberty to disclose to anyone the nature and content of any communication made with a view to and in connection with a friendly settlement. The second paragraph does not mean that all other proceedings shall not be confidential (see Article 40, paragraph 2). Details are to be specified in the rules of the Court.

94 Experience demonstrates the great utility of the conciliation element in Convention proceedings. Friendly settlement negotiations could be "guided", or even encouraged, by a judge (with the help of the registry of the Court). Also, during friendly settlement negotiations, parties may call upon the services of the Court's registry to help them in these negotiations. A member of a Chamber might at any stage assist the parties in settling their case.

Article 39 – Finding of a friendly settlement

95 The text of Article 39 is modelled on Rule 49, paragraph 2, of the former Rules of Court. The second part of this Article is virtually identical to the last sentence of paragraph 2 of former Article 28 of the Convention.

Article 40 – Public hearings and access to documents

96 The two paragraphs of Article 40 are modelled on, respectively, Rules 18 and 56, paragraph 2, of the former Rules of Court. The text thus indicates that proceedings, where oral, are, in principle, to be conducted in public. It also specifies that documents submitted in the written proceedings (memorials and formal written information) are also, in principle, accessible to the public. Thus, documents deposited with the Registrar and not published will be accessible to the public unless otherwise decided by the President either on his own initiative or at the request of a party, or of any other person concerned.

Article 41 – Just satisfaction

97 The text of Article 41 is a simplified and shortened version of former Article 50 of the Convention.

Article 42 – Judgments of Chambers

98 The Chamber will decide, as the Court had done in the past, by means of a judgment. This judgment will not – contrary to the former system – be immediately definitive, but will become so later in accordance with Article 44, paragraph 2. The judgment will have to be reasoned (Article 45, paragraph 1). It shall be transmitted to the parties but will not be published until

it has become final (Article 44, paragraph 3). Further details may be determined in the rules of the Court.

Articles 43 and 44 – Referral to the Grand Chamber and final judgments

99   A re-hearing of the case, as envisaged in Article 43, shall take place only exceptionally when a case raises a serious question affecting the interpretation or application of the Convention or a serious issue of general importance (see also paragraph 47 above). These conditions are taken, in part, from Article 5, paragraph 2, sub-paragraph 2, of Protocol No. 9 to the Convention. (At the time of entry into force of this Protocol, Protocol No. 9 to the Convention is repealed: see below and Article 2.) The intention is that these conditions will be applied in a strict sense.

100   Serious questions affecting the interpretation of the Convention are raised when a question of importance not yet decided by the Court is at stake, or when the decision is of importance for future cases and for the development of the Court's case-law. Moreover, a serious question may be particularly evident when the judgment concerned is not consistent with a previous judgment of the Court.

101   A serious question concerning the application of the Convention may be at stake when a judgment necessitates a substantial change to national law or administrative practice but does not itself raise a serious question of interpretation of the Convention.

102   A serious issue considered to be of general importance could involve a substantial political issue or an important issue of policy.

103   The parties to the case may request that the case be referred to the Grand Chamber within three months from the date of the judgment of the Chamber. In order to ensure that the parties are in a position to observe this time limit, they must be informed about the date on which the judgment is delivered. Modalities relating to the delivery and swift transmission of judgments to the parties need to be specified in the Court's rules. If the conditions for a referral are met, a panel of five judges of the Grand Chamber accepts the case and the Grand Chamber has to make the final determination as to whether the Convention has been violated after written and, if the Court so decides, oral proceedings. If these conditions are not met, the panel rejects the request and the Chamber's judgment becomes final (Article 44, paragraph 2.c).

104   Article 44, paragraph 1, is taken from former Article 52 of the Convention. Only judgments of the Grand Chamber are final, with immediate effect. The judgments of Chambers become final under conditions set out in paragraph 2. These judgments shall be published when they have become final; all judgments are accessible to the public.

The registry of the Court is to ensure all necessary arrangements relating to the transmission of judgments.

Article 45 – Reasons for judgments and decisions

105 Article 45, which is modelled on former Article 51 of the Convention, lays down a general rule that all judgments and most decisions of the Court must be reasoned, whether they relate to its jurisdiction, a question of procedure, the merits of the case or the award of just satisfaction to the applicant. It is understood that reasons for decisions rejecting or accepting applications can be given in summary form.

This article does not concern decisions taken by the panel of five judges of the Grand Chamber in accordance with Article 43.

Article 46 – Binding force and execution of judgments

106 Article 46 regroups Articles 53 and 54 of the former text of the Convention, no change of substance being involved. (The word "decision" is replaced by "judgment" in the first paragraph.)

The Committee of Ministers supervises the execution of judgments.

Articles 47, 48 and 49 – Advisory opinions

107 These articles are virtually identical to Articles 1, 2 and 3, paragraphs 2 to 4, of former Protocol No. 2 to the Convention. The words "two-thirds" have been deleted in paragraph 3 of Article 47 to take into account the change made by Protocol No. 10 with respect to former Article 32 of the Convention. As to Article 3, paragraph 1, of Protocol No. 2, consult Article 31 and paragraph 81 above.

108 Since Protocol No. 2 referred, in Article 1, paragraph 2, to the Commission, the present text needed appropriate amendment. It was considered more appropriate to incorporate Protocol No. 2 into the body of Protocol No. 11 rather than to amend the former.

Article 50 – Expenditure on the Court

109 Article 50 follows closely the text of former Article 58 of the Convention. The "expenditure" on the new Court will include, in addition to items relating to staff and equipment, the salaries and social security contributions which will be paid to or for the judges in lieu of the allowances provided for in former Article 42 of the Convention.

Article 51 – Privileges and immunities of judges

110 The text of Article 51 follows closely former Article 59 of the Convention.

111 The word "agreements" refers to the Fourth Protocol to the General Agreement on Privileges and Immunities of the Council of Europe and any further treaties ratified by States Parties on related subjects.

Article 2 of the amending Protocol – Replacement, deletion and amendment

112 Article 2 indicates which other provisions are replaced, deleted or amended by this Protocol.

113 The text of Article 56 repeats former Article 63 of the Convention. Paragraph 1 of this Article enables States to extend the Convention to territories for whose international relations States are responsible. Paragraph 4 enables States to make declarations in respect of territories accepting the competence of the Court to receive individual applications. Such declarations may be made for a specific period (the same applies to any similar declarations under Protocols Nos. 4 and 7). The provision in paragraph 3, that regard should be had to local requirements, is retained. The only changes of importance that have been made to the former Article 63 of the Convention (now Article 56) are that the words "subject to paragraph 4" have been added to paragraph 1 and that the word "Commission" is replaced by "Court" in paragraph 4. (See also paragraph 75, above.)

114 Headings have been included in order to facilitate comprehension of the text. As a consequence, and for the sake of consistency, this Article extends the insertion of titles to sections and headings to all the other Articles in the Convention and its protocols.

The headings listed in the appendix form an integral part of the Convention and its protocols, as amended by the present Protocol. The inclusion of such headings should not be understood as an interpretation of the Articles themselves or as having any legal effect. These headings have been added in order to make the text of the Convention more easily understandable (cf the American Convention on Human Rights).

Article 3 of the amending Protocol – Signature and ratification

115 The text of Article 3 is one of the usual final clauses included in treaties and agreements prepared within the Council of Europe. It is identical, for instance, to Article 6 of Protocol No. 9 to the Convention.

This Protocol does not contain any provisions on reservations. By its very nature, this amending Protocol excludes the making of reservations.

Article 4 of the amending Protocol – Entry into force

116 The text of Article 4 is also one of the usual final clauses included in treaties and agreements prepared within the Council of Europe. The Protocol, which is an amending Protocol (see Section V, paragraphs 55 and 56 above), shall enter into force one year after the last ratification. The States

Parties, as well as the competent bodies of the Council of Europe, should take all necessary steps to set up the new Court immediately after the last ratification, and especially the election of new judges. The Court should also take measures concerning its organisation as early as possible, especially those mentioned in Article 26. The second sentence of Article 4 of the Protocol makes such preparatory measures possible.

Article 5 of the amending Protocol – Transitional provisions

117 This Article provides the necessary transitional provisions for applications, pending the present Protocol's entry into force.

118 Paragraph 1 specifies that the office of members of the former Court and Commission, as well as the Registrar and the Deputy Registrar, will terminate as soon as this Protocol enters into force. This is to prevent two courts operating at the same time. The Commission will nevertheless continue to exist for the additional period of one year, as specified in paragraph 3.

119 Paragraphs 2 to 4 deal with applications pending before the Commission. When they have not yet been declared admissible by the Commission, applications will be dealt with by the Court under the new system (paragraph 2). On the other hand it was deemed appropriate that applications already declared admissible should be finalised by members of the Commission under the former system (paragraph 3). As it was considered inappropriate for the Commission to continue its work many years after this Protocol's entry into force, paragraph 3 provides for a time-limit of one year. This period was deemed to be sufficient for members of the Commission to finalise admissible applications. Applications that cannot be completed during this time-limit are to be examined by the Court under the new system. As these applications will have already been declared admissible by the Commission, there will be no need for them to be examined by a committee of the Court.

It should be noted that paragraph 3, first sentence, stipulates that members of the Commission are to continue their work for one year after the entry into force of this Protocol, even if their term in office expired before that date. This will allow them to complete all work on cases declared admissible during that period. Since the office of members of the Commission expires at the entry into force of the present Protocol, those Commissioners elected as judges to the new Court may continue, at the same time, their Commission functions as provided in paragraph 3 of Article 5. Any vacancy which occurs in the Commission during this period may be filled in accordance with the former relevant provisions of the Convention, so that no Contracting Party need be without a Commissioner during the said period.

120 Paragraph 4 of Article 5 concerns cases in which the Commission adopts a report in the period of twelve months following the entry into force of Protocol No. 11. For such cases, the procedure for bringing cases before

the Court in the former Article 48 of the Convention (and Protocol No. 9, where applicable) shall apply. In other words, the Commission or a State Party – as well as the applicant if Protocol No. 9 is applicable – will have the right to refer a case to the new Court.

121 In order to avoid cases which have already been examined being dealt with at three levels, the panel of five judges of the new Court will decide whether the Grand Chamber or a Chamber is to decide the case.

122 Cases not referred to the new Court under this Article will be decided by the Committee of Ministers in accordance with former Article 32 of the Convention.

123 The former Court will cease to function at the date of entry into force of this Protocol. All cases pending before the former Court are to be transmitted to the Grand Chamber of the new Court.

124 Paragraph 6 provides that the Committee of Ministers is to continue to deal with cases which have not been transmitted to the Court under former Article 48 of the Convention. The Committee of Ministers will continue to deal with such cases under former Article 32 of the Convention, even after this Protocol has entered into effect, until such time as they are completed.

Article 6 of the amending Protocol – Declarations

125 This Article makes it clear that declarations made under former Articles 25 and 46 of the Convention in relation to the applicability of the Convention *ratione temporis* (see paragraphs 83 to 86 above) shall, *mutatis mutandis*, remain valid for the jurisdiction of the new Court.

126 Moreover, declarations made before the entry into force of this Protocol under paragraph 4 of former Article 63 of the Convention remain valid.

Article 7 of the amending Protocol – Notification

127 Article 7 is one of the usual final clauses in Council of Europe treaties and agreements. It is virtually identical, for instance, to Article 14 of Protocol No. 8 to the Convention.

Rules of the European Court of Human Rights

4 November 1998

The European Court of Human Rights,

Having regard to the Convention for the Protection of Human Rights and Fundamental Freedoms and the Protocols thereto,

Makes the present Rules:

Rule 1

(Definitions)

For the purposes of these Rules unless the context otherwise requires:

a the term "Convention" means the Convention for the Protection of Human Rights and Fundamental Freedoms and the Protocols thereto;

b the expression "plenary Court" means the European Court of Human Rights sitting in plenary session;

c the term "Grand Chamber" means the Grand Chamber of seventeen judges constituted in pursuance of Article 27 § 1 of the Convention;

d the term "Section" means a Chamber set up by the plenary Court for a fixed period in pursuance of Article 26 (b) of the Convention and the expression "President of the Section" means the judge elected by the plenary Court in pursuance of Article 26 (c) of the Convention as President of such a Section;

e the term "Chamber" means any Chamber of seven judges constituted in pursuance of Article 27 § 1 of the Convention and the expression "President of the Chamber" means the judge presiding over such a "Chamber";

f the term "Committee" means a Committee of three judges set up in pursuance of Article 27 § 1 of the Convention;

g the term "Court" means either the plenary Court, the Grand Chamber, a Section, a Chamber, a Committee or the panel of five judges referred to in Article 43 § 2 of the Convention;

h the expression "*ad hoc* judge" means any person, other than an elected judge, chosen by a Contracting Party in pursuance of Article 27 § 2 of the Convention to sit as a member of the Grand Chamber or as a member of a Chamber;

i the terms "judge" and "judges" mean the judges elected by the Parliamentary Assembly of the Council of Europe or ad hoc judges;

j the term "Judge Rapporteur" means a judge appointed to carry out the tasks provided for in Rules 48 and 49;

k the term "Registrar" denotes the Registrar of the Court or the Registrar of a Section according to the context;

l the terms "party" and "parties" mean

the applicant or respondent Contracting Parties;

the applicant (the person, non-governmental organisation or group of individuals) that lodged a complaint under Article 34 of the Convention;

m the expression "third party" means any Contracting State or any person concerned who, as provided for in Article 36 §§ 1 and 2 of the Convention, has exercised its right or been invited to submit written comments or take part in a hearing;

n the expression "Committee of Ministers" means the Committee of Ministers of the Council of Europe;

o the terms "former Court" and "Commission" mean respectively the European Court and European Commission of Human Rights set up under former Article 19 of the Convention.

Title I – Organisation and working of the Court

Chapter I – Judges

Rule 2

(Calculation of term of office)

1   The duration of the term of office of an elected judge shall be calculated as from the date of election. However, when a judge is re-elected on the expiry of the term of office or is elected to replace a judge whose term of office has expired or is about to expire, the duration of the term of office shall, in either case, be calculated as from the date of such expiry.

2   In accordance with Article 23 § 5 of the Convention, a judge elected to replace a judge whose term of office has not expired shall hold office for the remainder of the predecessor's term.

3   In accordance with Article 23 § 7 of the Convention, an elected judge shall hold office until a successor has taken the oath or made the declaration provided for in Rule 3.

Rule 3

(Oath or solemn declaration)

1   Before taking up office, each elected judge shall, at the first sitting of the plenary Court at which the judge is present or, in case of need, before the President of the Court, take the following oath or make the following solemn declaration:

> "I swear" – or "I solemnly declare" – "that I will exercise my functions as a judge honourably, independently and impartially and that I will keep secret all deliberations."

2   This act shall be recorded in minutes.

Rule 4

(Incompatible activities)

In accordance with Article 21 § 3 of the Convention, the judges shall not during their term of office engage in any political or administrative activity or any professional activity which is incompatible with their independence or impartiality or with the demands of a full-time office. Each judge shall declare to the President of the Court any additional activity. In the event of a disagreement between the President and the judge concerned, any question arising shall be decided by the plenary Court.

Rule 5

(Precedence)

1   Elected judges shall take precedence after the President and Vice-Presidents of the Court and the Presidents of the Sections, according to the date of their election; in the event of re-election, even if it is not an immediate re-election, the length of time during which the judge concerned previously held office as a judge shall be taken into account.

2   Vice-Presidents of the Court elected to office on the same date shall take precedence according to the length of time they have served as judges. If the length of time they have served as judges is the same, they shall take precedence according to age. The same Rule shall apply to Presidents of Sections.

3   Judges who have served the same length of time as judges shall take precedence according to age.

4   *Ad hoc* judges shall take precedence after the elected judges according to age.

Rule 6

(Resignation)

Resignation of a judge shall be notified to the President of the Court, who shall transmit it to the Secretary General of the Council of Europe. Subject to the provisions of Rules 24 § 3 in fine and 26 § 2, resignation shall constitute vacation of office.

Rule 7

(Dismissal from office)

No judge may be dismissed from his or her office unless the other judges, meeting in plenary session, decide by a majority of two-thirds of the elected judges in office that he or she has ceased to fulfil the required conditions. He or she must first be heard by the plenary Court. Any judge may set in motion the procedure for dismissal from office.

Chapter II – Presidency of the Court

Rule 8

(Election of the President and Vice-Presidents of the Court and the Presidents and Vice-Presidents of the Sections)

1   The plenary Court shall elect its President, two Vice-Presidents and the Presidents of the Sections for a period of three years, provided that such period shall not exceed the duration of their terms of office as judges. They may be re-elected.

2   Each Section shall likewise elect for a renewable period of three years a Vice-President, who shall replace the President of the Section if the latter is unable to carry out his or her duties.

3   The Presidents and Vice-Presidents shall continue to hold office until the election of their successors.

4   If a President or a Vice-President ceases to be a member of the Court or resigns from office before its normal expiry, the plenary Court or the relevant Section, as the case may be, shall elect a successor for the remainder of the term of that office.

5   The elections referred to in this Rule shall be by secret ballot; only the elected judges who are present shall take part. If no judge receives an absolute majority of the elected judges present, a ballot shall take place between the two judges who have received most votes. In the event of a tie, preference shall be given to the judge having precedence in accordance with Rule 5.

Rule 9

(Functions of the President of the Court)

1   The President of the Court shall direct the work and administration of the Court. The President shall represent the Court and, in particular, be responsible for its relations with the authorities of the Council of Europe.

2   The President shall preside at plenary meetings of the Court, meetings of the Grand Chamber and meetings of the panel of five judges.

The President shall not take part in the consideration of cases being heard by Chambers except where he or she is the judge elected in respect of a Contracting Party concerned.

Rule 10

(Functions of the Vice-Presidents of the Court)

The Vice-Presidents of the Court shall assist the President of the Court. They shall take the place of the President if the latter is unable to carry out his or her duties or the office of President is vacant, or at the request of the President. They shall also act as Presidents of Sections.

Rule 11

(Replacement of the President and the Vice-Presidents)

If the President and the Vice-Presidents of the Court are at the same time unable to carry out their duties or if their offices are at the same time vacant, the office of President of the Court shall be assumed by a President of a Section or, if none is available, by another elected judge, in accordance with the order of precedence provided for in Rule 5.

Rule 12

(Presidency of Sections and Chambers)

The Presidents of the Sections shall preside at the sittings of the Section and Chambers of which they are members. The Vice-Presidents of the Sections shall take their place if they are unable to carry out their duties or if the office of President of the Section concerned is vacant, or at the request of the President of the Section. Failing that, the judges of the Section and the Chambers shall take their place, in the order of precedence provided for in Rule 5.

Rule 13

(Inability to preside)

Judges of the Court may not preside in cases in which the Contracting Party of which they are nationals or in respect of which they were elected is a party.

Rule 14

(Balanced representation of the sexes)

In relation to the making of appointments governed by this and the following chapter of the present Rules, the Court shall pursue a policy aimed at securing a balanced representation of the sexes.

Chapter III – The Registry

Rule 15

(Election of the Registrar)

1   The plenary Court shall elect its Registrar. The candidates shall be of high moral character and must possess the legal, managerial and linguistic knowledge and experience necessary to carry out the functions attaching to the post.

2   The Registrar shall be elected for a term of five years and may be re-elected. The Registrar may not be dismissed from office, unless the judges, meeting in plenary session, decide by a majority of two-thirds of the elected judges in office that the person concerned has ceased to fulfil the required conditions. He or she must first be heard by the plenary Court. Any judge may set in motion the procedure for dismissal from office.

3   The elections referred to in this Rule shall be by secret ballot; only the elected judges who are present shall take part. If no candidate receives an absolute majority of the elected judges present, a ballot shall take place between the two candidates who have received most votes. In the event of a tie, preference shall be given, firstly, to the female candidate, if any, and, secondly, to the older candidate.

4   Before taking up office, the Registrar shall take the following oath or make the following solemn declaration before the plenary Court or, if need be, before the President of the Court:

"I swear" – or "I solemnly declare" – "that I will exercise loyally, discreetly and conscientiously the functions conferred upon me as Registrar of the European Court of Human Rights."

This act shall be recorded in minutes.

Rule 16

(Election of the Deputy Registrars)

1   The plenary Court shall also elect two Deputy Registrars on the conditions and in the manner and for the term prescribed in the preceding Rule. The procedure for dismissal from office provided for in respect of the Registrar shall likewise apply. The Court shall first consult the Registrar in both these matters.

2   Before taking up office, a Deputy Registrar shall take an oath or make a solemn declaration before the plenary Court or, if need be, before the President of the Court, in terms similar to those prescribed in respect of the Registrar. This act shall be recorded in minutes.

Rule 17

(Functions of the Registrar)

1   The Registrar shall assist the Court in the performance of its functions and shall be responsible for the organisation and activities of the Registry under the authority of the President of the Court.

2   The Registrar shall have the custody of the archives of the Court and shall be the channel for all communications and notifications made by, or addressed to, the Court in connection with the cases brought or to be brought before it.

3   The Registrar shall, subject to the duty of discretion attaching to this office, reply to requests for information concerning the work of the Court, in particular to enquiries from the press.

4   General instructions drawn up by the Registrar, and approved by the President of the Court, shall regulate the working of the Registry.

Rule 18

(Organisation of the Registry)

1   The Registry shall consist of Section Registries equal to the number of Sections set up by the Court and of the departments necessary to provide the legal and administrative services required by the Court.

2   The Section Registrar shall assist the Section in the performance of its functions and may be assisted by a Deputy Section Registrar.

3   The officials of the Registry, including the legal secretaries but not the Registrar and the Deputy Registrars, shall be appointed by the Secretary General of the Council of Europe with the agreement of the President of the Court or of the Registrar acting on the President's instructions.

Chapter IV – The working of the Court

Rule 19

(Seat of the Court)

1   The seat of the Court shall be at the seat of the Council of Europe at Strasbourg. The Court may, however, if it considers it expedient, perform its functions elsewhere in the territories of the member States of the Council of Europe.

2   The Court may decide, at any stage of the examination of an application, that it is necessary that an investigation or any other function be carried out elsewhere by it or one or more of its members.

Rule 20

(Sessions of the plenary Court)

1   The plenary sessions of the Court shall be convened by the President of the Court whenever the performance of its functions under the Convention and under these Rules so requires. The President of the Court shall convene a plenary session if at least one-third of the members of the Court so request, and in any event once a year to consider administrative matters.

2   The quorum of the plenary Court shall be two-thirds of the elected judges in office.

3   If there is no quorum, the President shall adjourn the sitting.

Rule 21

(Other sessions of the Court)

1   The Grand Chamber, the Chambers and the Committees shall sit full time. On a proposal by the President, however, the Court shall fix session periods each year.

2   Outside those periods the Grand Chamber and the Chambers shall be convened by their Presidents in cases of urgency.

Rule 22

(Deliberations)

1   The Court shall deliberate in private. Its deliberations shall remain secret.

2   Only the judges shall take part in the deliberations. The Registrar or the designated substitute, as well as such other officials of the Registry and interpreters whose assistance is deemed necessary, shall be present. No other person may be admitted except by special decision of the Court.

3   Before a vote is taken on any matter in the Court, the President may request the judges to state their opinions on it.

Rule 23

(Votes)

1   The decisions of the Court shall be taken by a majority of the judges present. In the event of a tie, a fresh vote shall be taken and, if there is still a tie, the President shall have a casting vote. This paragraph shall apply unless otherwise provided for in these Rules.

2   The decisions and judgments of the Grand Chamber and the Chambers shall be adopted by a majority of the sitting judges. Abstentions shall not be allowed in final votes on the admissibility and merits of cases.

3   As a general rule, votes shall be taken by a show of hands. The President may take a roll-call vote, in reverse order of precedence.

4   Any matter that is to be voted upon shall be formulated in precise terms.

Chapter V – The Chambers

Rule 24

(Composition of the Grand Chamber)

1   The Grand Chamber shall be composed of seventeen judges and three substitute judges.

2   The Grand Chamber shall be constituted for three years with effect from the election of the presidential office-holders referred to in Rule 8.

3   The Grand Chamber shall include the President and Vice-Presidents of the Court and the Presidents of the Sections. In order to complete the Grand Chamber, the plenary Court shall, on a proposal by its President, divide all the other judges into two groups which shall alternate every nine months and whose membership shall be geographically as balanced as possible and reflect the different legal systems among the Contracting Parties. The judges and substitute judges who are to hear each case referred to the Grand Chamber during each nine-month period shall be designated in rotation within each group; they shall remain members of the Grand Chamber until the proceedings have been completed, even after their terms of office as judges have expired.

4   If he or she does not sit as a member of the Grand Chamber by virtue of paragraph 3 of the present Rule, the judge elected in respect of any Contracting Party concerned shall sit as an ex officio member of the Grand Chamber in accordance with Article 27 §§ 2 and 3 of the Convention.

5   a Where any President of a Section is unable to sit as a member of the Grand Chamber, he or she shall be replaced by the Vice-President of the Section.

b If other judges are prevented from sitting, they shall be replaced by the substitute judges in the order in which the latter were selected under paragraph 3 of the present Rule.

c If there are not enough substitute judges in the group concerned to complete the Grand Chamber, the substitute judges lacking shall be designated by a drawing of lots amongst the members of the other group.

6   a The panel of five judges of the Grand Chamber called upon to consider requests submitted under Article 43 of the Convention shall be composed of

– the President of the Court,

– the Presidents or, if they are prevented from sitting, the Vice-Presidents of the Sections other than the Section from which was constituted the Chamber that dealt with the case whose referral to the Grand Chamber is being sought,

– one further judge designated in rotation from among the judges other than those who dealt with the case in the Chamber.

b No judge elected in respect of, or who is a national of, a Contracting Party concerned may be a member of the panel.

c Any member of the panel unable to sit shall be replaced by another judge who did not deal with the case in the Chamber, who shall be designated in rotation.

Rule 25

(Setting up of Sections)

1   The Chambers provided for in Article 26 (b) of the Convention (referred to in these Rules as "Sections") shall be set up by the plenary Court, on a proposal by its President, for a period of three years with effect from the election of the presidential office-holders of the Court under Rule 8. There shall be at least four Sections.

2   Each judge shall be a member of a Section. The composition of the Sections shall be geographically and gender balanced and shall reflect the different legal systems among the Contracting Parties.

3   Where a judge ceases to be a member of the Court before the expiry of the period for which the Section has been constituted, the judge's place in the Section shall be taken by his or her successor as a member of the Court.

4   The President of the Court may exceptionally make modifications to the composition of the Sections if circumstances so require.

5   On a proposal by the President, the plenary Court may constitute an additional Section.

Rule 26

(Constitution of Chambers)

1   The Chambers of seven judges provided for in Article 27 § 1 of the Convention for the consideration of cases brought before the Court shall be constituted from the Sections as follows.

a The Chamber shall in each case include the President of the Section and the judge elected in respect of any Contracting Party concerned. If the latter judge is not a member of the Section to which the application has been assigned under Rule 51 or 52, he or she shall sit as an ex officio member of the Chamber in accordance with Article 27 § 2 of the Convention. Rule 29 shall apply if that judge is unable to sit or withdraws.

b The other members of the Chamber shall be designated by the President of the Section in rotation from among the members of the relevant Section.

c The members of the Section who are not so designated shall sit in the case as substitute judges.

2   Even after the end of their terms of office judges shall continue to deal with cases in which they have participated in the consideration of the merits.

Rule 27

(Committees)

1   Committees composed of three judges belonging to the same Section shall be set up under Article 27 § 1 of the Convention. After consulting the Presidents of the Sections, the President of the Court shall decide on the number of Committees to be set up.

2   The Committees shall be constituted for a period of twelve months by rotation among the members of each Section, excepting the President of the Section.

3   The judges of the Section who are not members of a Committee may be called upon to take the place of members who are unable to sit.

4   Each Committee shall be chaired by the member having precedence in the Section.

Rule 28

(Inability to sit, withdrawal or exemption)

1   Any judge who is prevented from taking part in sittings shall, as soon as possible, give notice to the President of the Chamber.

2   A judge may not take part in the consideration of any case in which he or she has a personal interest or has previously acted either as the Agent, advocate or adviser of a party or of a person having an interest in the case, or as a member of a tribunal or commission of inquiry, or in any other capacity.

3   If a judge withdraws for one of the said reasons, or for some special reason, he or she shall inform the President of the Chamber, who shall exempt the judge from sitting.

4   If the President of the Chamber considers that a reason exists for a judge to withdraw, he or she shall consult with the judge concerned; in the event of disagreement, the Chamber shall decide.

Rule 29

(Ad hoc judges)

1   If the judge elected in respect of a Contracting Party concerned is unable to sit in the Chamber or withdraws, the President of the Chamber shall invite that Party to indicate within thirty days whether it wishes to appoint to sit as judge either another elected judge or, as an ad hoc judge, any other person possessing the qualifications required by Article 21 § 1 of the Convention and, if so, to state at the same time the name of the person appointed. The same rule shall apply if the person so appointed is unable to sit or withdraws.

2   The Contracting Party concerned shall be presumed to have waived its right of appointment if it does not reply within thirty days.

3   An ad hoc judge shall, at the opening of the first sitting fixed for the consideration of the case after the judge has been appointed, take the oath or make the solemn declaration provided for in Rule 3. This act shall be recorded in minutes.

Rule 30

(Common interest)

1   If several applicant or respondent Contracting Parties have a common interest, the President of the Court may invite them to agree to appoint a single elected judge or ad hoc judge in accordance with Article 27 § 2 of the Convention. If the Parties are unable to agree, the President shall choose by lot, from among the persons proposed as judges by these Parties, the judge called upon to sit ex officio.

2   In the event of a dispute as to the existence of a common interest, the plenary Court shall decide.

Title II – Procedure

Chapter I – General Rules

Rule 31

(Possibility of particular derogations)

The provisions of this Title shall not prevent the Court from derogating from them for the consideration of a particular case after having consulted the parties where appropriate.

Rule 32

(Practice directions)

The President of the Court may issue practice directions, notably in relation to such matters as appearance at hearings and the filing of pleadings and other documents.

Rule 33

(Public character of proceedings)

1   Hearings shall be public unless, in accordance with paragraph 2 of this Rule, the Chamber in exceptional circumstances decides otherwise, either of its own motion or at the request of a party or any other person concerned.

2   The press and the public may be excluded from all or part of a hearing in the interest of morals, public order or national security in a democratic society, where the interests of juveniles or the protection of the private life of the parties so require, or to the extent strictly necessary in the opinion of the Chamber in special circumstances where publicity would prejudice the interests of justice.

3   Following registration of an application, all documents deposited with the Registry, with the exception of those deposited within the framework of friendly-settlement negotiations as provided for in Rule 62, shall be accessible to the public unless the President of the Chamber, for the reasons set out in paragraph 2 of this Rule, decides otherwise, either of his or her own motion or at the request of a party or any other person concerned.

4   Any request for confidentiality made under paragraphs 1 or 3 above must give reasons and specify whether the hearing or the documents, as the case may be, should be inaccessible to the public in whole or in part.

Rule 34

(Use of languages)

1   The official languages of the Court shall be English and French.

2   Before the decision on the admissibility of an application is taken, all communications with and pleadings by applicants under Article 34 of the Convention or their representatives, if not in one of the Court's official languages, shall be in one of the official languages of the Contracting Parties.

3   a All communications with and pleadings by such applicants or their representatives in respect of a hearing, or after a case has been declared admissible, shall be in one of the Court's official languages, unless the President of the Chamber authorises the continued use of the official language of a Contracting Party.

b If such leave is granted, the Registrar shall make the necessary arrangements for the oral or written translation of the applicant's observations or statements.

4   a All communications with and pleadings by Contracting Parties or third parties shall be in one of the Court's official languages. The President of the Chamber may authorise the use of a non-official language.

b   If such leave is granted, it shall be the responsibility of the requesting party to provide for and bear the costs of interpreting or translation into English or French of the oral arguments or written statements made.

5   The President of the Chamber may invite the respondent Contracting Party to provide a translation of its written submissions in the or an official language of that Party in order to facilitate the applicant's understanding of those submissions.

6   Any witness, expert or other person appearing before the Court may use his or her own language if he or she does not have sufficient knowledge of either of the two official languages. In that event the Registrar shall make the necessary arrangements for interpreting or translation.

Rule 35

(Representation of Contracting Parties)

The Contracting Parties shall be represented by Agents, who may have the assistance of advocates or advisers.

Rule 36

(Representation of applicants)

1   Persons, non-governmental organisations or groups of individuals may initially present applications under Article 34 of the Convention themselves or through a representative appointed under paragraph 4 of this Rule.

2   Following notification of the application to the respondent Contracting Party under Rule 54 § 3 (b), the President of the Chamber may direct that the applicant should be represented in accordance with paragraph 4 of this Rule.

3   The applicant must be so represented at any hearing decided on by the Chamber or for the purposes of the proceedings following a decision to declare the application admissible, unless the President of the Chamber decides otherwise.

4   a   The representative of the applicant shall be an advocate authorised to practise in any of the Contracting Parties and resident in the territory of one of them, or any other person approved by the President of the Chamber.

b   The President of the Chamber may, where representation would otherwise be obligatory, grant leave to the applicant to present his or her own case, subject, if necessary, to being assisted by an advocate or other approved representative.

c   In exceptional circumstances and at any stage of the procedure, the President of the Chamber may, where he or she considers that the circumstances or the conduct of the advocate or other person appointed under the preceding sub-paragraphs so warrant, direct that the latter may no longer represent or assist the applicant and that the applicant should seek alternative representation.

5   The advocate or other approved representative, or the applicant in person if he or she seeks leave to present his or her own case, must have an adequate knowledge of one of the Court's official languages. However, leave to use a non-official language may be given by the President of the Chamber under Rule 34 § 3.

Rule 37

(Communications, notifications and summonses)

1   Communications or notifications addressed to the Agents or advocates of the parties shall be deemed to have been addressed to the parties.

2   If, for any communication, notification or summons addressed to persons other than the Agents or advocates of the parties, the Court considers it necessary to have the assistance of the Government of the State on whose territory such communication, notification or summons is to have effect, the

President of the Court shall apply directly to that Government in order to obtain the necessary facilities.

3   The same rule shall apply when the Court desires to make or arrange for the making of an investigation on the spot in order to establish the facts or to procure evidence or when it orders the appearance of a person who is resident in, or will have to cross, that territory.

Rule 38

(Written pleadings)

1   No written observations or other documents may be filed after the time-limit set by the President of the Chamber or the Judge Rapporteur, as the case may be, in accordance with these Rules. No written observations or other documents filed outside that time-limit or contrary to any practice direction issued under Rule 32 shall be included in the case file unless the President of the Chamber decides otherwise.

2   For the purposes of observing the time-limit referred to in paragraph 1, the material date is the certified date of dispatch of the document or, if there is none, the actual date of receipt at the Registry.

Rule 39

(Interim measures)

1   The Chamber or, where appropriate, its President may, at the request of a party or of any other person concerned, or of its own motion, indicate to the parties any interim measure which it considers should be adopted in the interests of the parties or of the proper conduct of the proceedings before it.

2   Notice of these measures shall be given to the Committee of Ministers.

3   The Chamber may request information from the parties on any matter connected with the implementation of any interim measure it has indicated.

Rule 40

(Urgent notification of an application)

In any case of urgency the Registrar, with the authorisation of the President of the Chamber, may, without prejudice to the taking of any other procedural steps and by any available means, inform a Contracting Party concerned in an application of the introduction of the application and of a summary of its objects.

Rule 41

(Case priority)

The Chamber shall deal with applications in the order in which they become ready for examination. It may, however, decide to give priority to a particular application.

Rule 42

(Measures for taking evidence)

1   The Chamber may, at the request of a party or a third party, or of its own motion, obtain any evidence which it considers capable of providing clarification of the facts of the case. The Chamber may, inter alia, request the parties to produce documentary evidence and decide to hear as a witness or expert or in any other capacity any person whose evidence or statements seem likely to assist it in the carrying out of its tasks.

2   The Chamber may, at any time during the proceedings, depute one or more of its members or of the other judges of the Court to conduct an inquiry, carry out an investigation on the spot or take evidence in some other manner. It may appoint independent external experts to assist such a delegation.

3   The Chamber may ask any person or institution of its choice to obtain information, express an opinion or make a report on any specific point.

4   The parties shall assist the Chamber, or its delegation, in implementing any measures for taking evidence.

5   Where a report has been drawn up or some other measure taken in accordance with the preceding paragraphs at the request of an applicant or respondent Contracting Party, the costs entailed shall be borne by that Party unless the Chamber decides otherwise. In other cases the Chamber shall decide whether such costs are to be borne by the Council of Europe or awarded against the applicant or third party at whose request the report was drawn up or the other measure was taken. In all cases the costs shall be taxed by the President of the Chamber.

Rule 43

(Joinder and simultaneous examination of applications)

1   The Chamber may, either at the request of the parties or of its own motion, order the joinder of two or more applications.

2   The President of the Chamber may, after consulting the parties, order that the proceedings in applications assigned to the same Chamber be conducted simultaneously, without prejudice to the decision of the Chamber on the joinder of the applications.

Rule 44

(Striking out and restoration to the list)

1   When an applicant Contracting Party notifies the Registrar of its intention not to proceed with the case, the Chamber may strike the application out of the Court's list under Article 37 of the Convention if the other Contracting Party or Parties concerned in the case agree to such discontinuance.

2   The decision to strike out an application which has been declared admissible shall be given in the form of a judgment. The President of the Chamber shall forward that judgment, once it has become final, to the Committee of Ministers in order to allow the latter to supervise, in accordance with Article 46 § 2 of the Convention, the execution of any undertakings which may have been attached to the discontinuance, friendly settlement or solution of the matter.

3   When an application has been struck out, the costs shall be at the discretion of the Court. If an award of costs is made in a decision striking out an application which has not been declared admissible, the President of the Chamber shall forward the decision to the Committee of Ministers

4   The Court may restore an application to its list if it concludes that exceptional circumstances justify such a course.

Chapter II – Institution of proceedings

Rule 45

(Signatures)

1   Any application made under Articles 33 or 34 of the Convention shall be submitted in writing and shall be signed by the applicant or by the applicant's representative.

2   Where an application is made by a non-governmental organisation or by a group of individuals, it shall be signed by those persons competent to represent that organisation or group. The Chamber or Committee concerned shall determine any question as to whether the persons who have signed an application are competent to do so.

3   Where applicants are represented in accordance with Rule 36, a power of attorney or written authority to act shall be supplied by their representative or representatives.

Rule 46

(Contents of an inter-State application)

Any Contracting Party or Parties intending to bring a case before the Court under Article 33 of the Convention shall file with the registry an application setting out

a the name of the Contracting Party against which the application is made;

b a statement of the facts;

c a statement of the alleged violation(s) of the Convention and the relevant arguments;

d a statement on compliance with the admissibility criteria (exhaustion of domestic remedies and the six-month rule) laid down in Article 35 § 1 of the Convention;

e the object of the application and a general indication of any claims for just satisfaction made under Article 41 of the Convention on behalf of the alleged injured party or parties; and

f the name and address of the person(s) appointed as Agent; and accompanied by

g copies of any relevant documents and in particular the decisions, whether judicial or not, relating to the object of the application.

Rule 47

(Contents of an individual application)

1 Any application under Article 34 of the Convention shall be made on the application form provided by the registry, unless the President of the Section concerned decides otherwise. It shall set out

a the name, date of birth, nationality, sex, occupation and address of the applicant;

b the name, occupation and address of the representative, if any;

c the name of the Contracting Party or Parties against which the application is made;

d a succinct statement of the facts;

e a succinct statement of the alleged violation(s) of the Convention and the relevant arguments;

f a succinct statement on the applicant's compliance with the admissibility criteria (exhaustion of domestic remedies and the six-month rule) laid down in Article 35 § 1 of the Convention; and

g the object of the application as well as a general indication of any claims for just satisfaction which the applicant may wish to make under Article 41 of the Convention;

and be accompanied by

h copies of any relevant documents and in particular the decisions, whether judicial or not, relating to the object of the application.

2   Applicants shall furthermore

a provide information, notably the documents and decisions referred to in paragraph 1 h above, enabling it to be shown that the admissibility criteria (exhaustion of domestic remedies and the six-month rule) laid down in Article 35 § 1 of the Convention have been satisfied; and

b indicate whether they have submitted their complaints to any other procedure of international investigation or settlement.

3   Applicants who do not wish their identity to be disclosed to the public shall so indicate and shall submit a statement of the reasons justifying such a departure from the normal rule of public access to information in proceedings before the Court. The President of the Chamber may authorise anonymity in exceptional and duly justified cases.

Failure to comply with the requirements set out in paragraphs 1 and 2 above may result in the application not being registered and examined by the Court.

5   The date of introduction of the application shall as a general rule be considered to be the date of the first communication from the applicant setting out, even summarily, the object of the application. The Court may for good cause nevertheless decide that a different date shall be considered to be the date of introduction.

6   Applicants shall keep the Court informed of any change of address and of all circumstances relevant to the application.

Chapter III – Judge Rapporteurs

Rule 48

(Inter-State applications)

1   Where an application is made under Article 33 of the Convention, the Chamber constituted to consider the case shall designate one or more of its judges as Judge Rapporteur(s), who shall submit a report on admissibility when the written observations of the Contracting Parties concerned have been received. Rule 49 § 4 shall, in so far as appropriate, be applicable to this report.

2   After an application made under Article 33 of the Convention has been declared admissible, the Judge Rapporteur(s) shall submit such reports, drafts and other documents as may assist the Chamber in the carrying out of its functions.

Rule 49

(Individual applications)

1   Where an application is made under Article 34 of the Convention, the President of the Section to which the case has been assigned shall designate a judge as Judge Rapporteur, who shall examine the application.

2   In their examination of applications Judge Rapporteurs

a may request the parties to submit, within a specified time, any factual information, documents or other material which they consider to be relevant;

b shall, subject to the President of the Section directing that the case be considered by a Chamber, decide whether the application is to be considered by a Committee or by a Chamber.

3   Where a case is considered by a Committee in accordance with Article 28 of the Convention, the report of the Judge Rapporteur shall contain

a a brief statement of the relevant facts;

b a brief statement of the reasons underlying the proposal to declare the application inadmissible or to strike it out of the list.

4   Where a case is considered by a Chamber pursuant to Article 29 § 1 of the Convention, the report of the Judge Rapporteur shall contain

a a statement of the relevant facts, including any information obtained under paragraph 2 of this Rule;

b an indication of the issues arising under the Convention in the application;

c a proposal on admissibility and on any other action to be taken, together, if need be, with a provisional opinion on the merits.

5   After an application made under Article 34 of the Convention has been declared admissible, the Judge Rapporteur shall submit such reports, drafts and other documents as may assist the Chamber in the carrying out of its functions.

Rule 50

(Grand Chamber proceedings)

Where a case has been submitted to the Grand Chamber either under Article 30 or under Article 43 of the Convention, the President of the Grand Chamber shall designate as Judge Rapporteur(s) one or, in the case of an inter-State application, one or more of its members.

Chapter IV – Proceedings on admissibility

Inter-State applications

Rule 51

1   When an application is made under Article 33 of the Convention, the President of the Court shall immediately give notice of the application to the respondent Contracting Party and shall assign the application to one of the Sections.

2   In accordance with Rule 26 § 1 (a), the judges elected in respect of the applicant and respondent Contracting Parties shall sit as ex officio members of the Chamber constituted to consider the case. Rule 30 shall apply if the application has been brought by several Contracting Parties or if applications with the same object brought by several Contracting Parties are being examined jointly under Rule 43 § 2.

3   On assignment of the case to a Section, the President of the Section shall constitute the Chamber in accordance with Rule 26 § 1 and shall invite the respondent Contracting Party to submit its observations in writing on the admissibility of the application. The observations so obtained shall be communicated by the Registrar to the applicant Contracting Party, which may submit written observations in reply.

4   Before ruling on the admissibility of the application, the Chamber may decide to invite the parties to submit further observations in writing.

5   A hearing on the admissibility shall be held if one or more of the Contracting Parties concerned so requests or if the Chamber so decides of its own motion.

6   After consulting the Parties, the President of the Chamber shall fix the written and, where appropriate, oral procedure and for that purpose shall lay down the time-limit within which any written observations are to be filed.

7   In its deliberations the Chamber shall take into consideration the report submitted by the Judge Rapporteur(s) under Rule 48 § 1.

Individual applications

Rule 52

(Assignment of applications to the Sections)

1   Any application made under Article 34 of the Convention shall be assigned to a Section by the President of the Court, who in so doing shall endeavour to ensure a fair distribution of cases between the Sections.

2   The Chamber of seven judges provided for in Article 27 § 1 of the Convention shall be constituted by the President of the Section concerned in

accordance with Rule 26 § 1 once it has been decided that the application is to be considered by a Chamber.

3   Pending the constitution of a Chamber in accordance with the preceding paragraph, the President of the Section shall exercise any powers conferred on the President of the Chamber by these Rules.

Rule 53

(Procedure before a Committee)

1   In its deliberations the Committee shall take into consideration the report submitted by the Judge Rapporteur under Rule 49 § 3.

2   The Judge Rapporteur, if he or she is not a member of the Committee, may be invited to attend the deliberations of the Committee.

3   In accordance with Article 28 of the Convention, the Committee may, by a unanimous vote, declare inadmissible or strike out of the Court's list of cases an application where such a decision can be taken without further examination. This decision shall be final.

4   If no decision pursuant to paragraph 3 of the present Rule is taken, the application shall be forwarded to the Chamber constituted under Rule 52 § 2 to examine the case.

Rule 54

(Procedure before a Chamber)

1   In its deliberations the Chamber shall take into consideration the report submitted by the Judge Rapporteur under Rule 49 § 4.

2   The Chamber may at once declare the application inadmissible or strike it out of the Court's list of cases.

3   Alternatively, the Chamber may decide to

    a request the parties to submit any factual information, documents or other material which it considers to be relevant;

    b give notice of the application to the respondent Contracting Party and invite that Party to submit written observations on the application;

    c invite the parties to submit further observations in writing.

4   Before taking its decision on admissibility, the Chamber may decide, either at the request of the parties or of its own motion, to hold a hearing. In that event, unless the Chamber shall exceptionally decide otherwise, the parties shall be invited also to address the issues arising in relation to the merits of the application.

5   The President of the Chamber shall fix the procedure, including time-limits, in relation to any decisions taken by the Chamber under paragraphs 3 and 4 of this Rule.

Inter-State and individual applications

Rule 55

(Pleas of inadmissibility)

Any plea of inadmissibility must, in so far as its character and the circumstances permit, be raised by the respondent Contracting Party in its written or oral observations on the admissibility of the application submitted as provided in Rule 51 or 54, as the case may be.

Rule 56

(Decision of a Chamber)

1   The decision of the Chamber shall state whether it was taken unanimously or by a majority and shall be accompanied or followed by reasons.

2   The decision of the Chamber shall be communicated by the Registrar to the applicant and to the Contracting Party or Parties concerned.

Rule 57

(Language of the decision)

1   Unless the Court decides that a decision shall be given in both official languages, all decisions shall be given either in English or in French. Decisions given shall be accessible to the public.

2   Publication of such decisions in the official reports of the Court, as provided for in Rule 78, shall be in both official languages of the Court.

Chapter V – Proceedings after the admission of an application

Rule 58

(Inter-State applications)

1   Once the Chamber has decided to admit an application made under Article 33 of the Convention, the President of the Chamber shall, after consulting the Contracting Parties concerned, lay down the time-limits for the filing of written observations on the merits and for the production of any further evidence. The President may however, with the agreement of the Contracting Parties concerned, direct that a written procedure is to be dispensed with.

2   A hearing on the merits shall be held if one or more of the Contracting Parties concerned so requests or if the Chamber so decides of its own motion. The President of the Chamber shall fix the oral procedure.

3   In its deliberations the Chamber shall take into consideration any reports, drafts and other documents submitted by the Judge Rapporteur(s) under Rule 48 § 2.

Rule 59

(Individual applications)

1   Once the Chamber has decided to admit an application made under Article 34 of the Convention, it may invite the parties to submit further evidence and written observations.

2   A hearing on the merits shall be held if the Chamber so decides of its own motion or, provided that no hearing also addressing the merits has been held at the admissibility stage under Rule 54 § 4, if one of the parties so requests. However, the Chamber may exceptionally decide that the discharging of its functions under Article 38 § 1 (a) of the Convention does not require a hearing to be held.

3   The President of the Chamber shall, where appropriate, fix the written and oral procedure.

4   In its deliberations the Chamber shall take into consideration any reports, drafts and other documents submitted by the Judge Rapporteur under Rule 49 § 5.

Rule 60

(Claims for just satisfaction)

1   Any claim which the applicant Contracting Party or the applicant may wish to make for just satisfaction under Article 41 of the Convention shall, unless the President of the Chamber directs otherwise, be set out in the written observations on the merits or, if no such written observations are filed, in a special document filed no later than two months after the decision declaring the application admissible.

2   Itemised particulars of all claims made, together with the relevant supporting documents or vouchers, shall be submitted, failing which the Chamber may reject the claim in whole or in part.

3   The Chamber may, at any time during the proceedings, invite any party to submit comments on the claim for just satisfaction.

Rule 61

(Third-party intervention)

1   The decision declaring an application admissible shall be notified by the Registrar to any Contracting Party one of whose nationals is an applicant in the case, as well as to the respondent Contracting Party under Rule 56 § 2.

2   Where a Contracting Party seeks to exercise its right to submit written comments or to take part in an oral hearing, pursuant to Article 36 § 1 of the Convention, the President of the Chamber shall fix the procedure to be followed.

3   In accordance with Article 36 § 2 of the Convention, the President of the Chamber may, in the interests of the proper administration of justice, invite or grant leave to any Contracting State which is not a party to the proceedings, or any person concerned who is not the applicant, to submit written comments or, in exceptional cases, to take part in an oral hearing. Requests for leave for this purpose must be duly reasoned and submitted in one of the official languages, within a reasonable time after the fixing of the written procedure.

4   Any invitation or grant of leave referred to in paragraph 3 of this Rule shall be subject to any conditions, including time-limits, set by the President of the Chamber. Where such conditions are not complied with, the President may decide not to include the comments in the case file.

5   Written comments submitted in accordance with this Rule shall be submitted in one of the official languages, save where leave to use another language has been granted under Rule 34 § 4. They shall be transmitted by the Registrar to the parties to the case, who shall be entitled, subject to any conditions, including time-limits, set by the President of the Chamber, to file written observations in reply.

Rule 62

(Friendly settlement)

1   Once an application has been declared admissible, the Registrar, acting on the instructions of the Chamber or its President, shall enter into contact with the parties with a view to securing a friendly settlement of the matter in accordance with Article 38 § 1 (b) of the Convention. The Chamber shall take any steps that appear appropriate to facilitate such a settlement.

2   In accordance with Article 38 § 2 of the Convention, the friendly settlement negotiations shall be confidential and without prejudice to the parties' arguments in the contentious proceedings. No written or oral communication and no offer or concession made in the framework of the attempt to secure a friendly settlement may be referred to or relied on in the contentious proceedings.

3   If the Chamber is informed by the Registrar that the parties have agreed to a friendly settlement, it shall, after verifying that the settlement has been reached on the basis of respect for human rights as defined in the Convention and the protocols thereto, strike the case out of the Court's list in accordance with Rule 44 § 2.

Chapter VI – Hearings

Rule 63

(Conduct of hearings)

1   The President of the Chamber shall direct hearings and shall prescribe the order in which Agents and advocates or advisers of the parties shall be called upon to speak.

2   Where a fact-finding hearing is being carried out by a delegation of the Chamber under Rule 42, the head of the delegation shall conduct the hearing and the delegation shall exercise any relevant power conferred on the Chamber by the Convention or these Rules.

Rule 64

(Failure to appear at a hearing)

Where, without showing sufficient cause, a party fails to appear, the Chamber may, provided that it is satisfied that such a course is consistent with the proper administration of justice, nonetheless proceed with the hearing.

Rule 65

(Convocation of witnesses, experts and other persons; costs of their appearance)

1   Witnesses, experts and other persons whom the Chamber or the President of the Chamber decides to hear shall be summoned by the Registrar.

2   The summons shall indicate

a   the case in connection with which it has been issued;

b   the object of the inquiry, expert opinion or other measure ordered by the Chamber or the President of the Chamber;

c   any provisions for the payment of the sum due to the person summoned.

3   If the persons concerned appear at the request or on behalf of an applicant or respondent Contracting Party, the costs of their appearance shall be borne by that Party unless the Chamber decides otherwise. In other cases, the Chamber shall decide whether such costs are to be borne by the Council of Europe or awarded against the applicant or third party at whose request the person summoned appeared. In all cases the costs shall be taxed by the President of the Chamber.

Rule 66

(Oath or solemn declaration by witnesses and experts)

1   After the establishment of the identity of the witness and before testifying, every witness shall take the following oath or make the following solemn declaration:

"I swear" – or "I solemnly declare upon my honour and conscience" – "that I shall speak the truth, the whole truth and nothing but the truth."

This act shall be recorded in minutes.

2   After the establishment of the identity of the expert and before carrying out his or her task, every expert shall take the following oath or make the following solemn declaration:

"I swear" – or "I solemnly declare" – "that I will discharge my duty as an expert honourably and conscientiously."

This act shall be recorded in minutes.

3   This oath may be taken or this declaration made before the President of the Chamber, or before a judge or any public authority nominated by the President.

Rule 67

(Objection to a witness or expert; hearing of a person for information purposes)

The Chamber shall decide in the event of any dispute arising from an objection to a witness or expert. It may hear for information purposes a person who cannot be heard as a witness.

Rule 68

(Questions put during hearings)

1   Any judge may put questions to the Agents, advocates or advisers of the parties, to the applicant, witnesses and experts, and to any other persons appearing before the Chamber.

2   The witnesses, experts and other persons referred to in Rule 42 § 1 may, subject to the control of the President of the Chamber, be examined by the Agents and advocates or advisers of the parties. In the event of an objection as to the relevance of a question put, the President of the Chamber shall decide.

Rule 69

(Failure to appear, refusal to give evidence or false evidence)

If, without good reason, a witness or any other person who has been duly summoned fails to appear or refuses to give evidence, the Registrar shall, on being so required by the President of the Chamber, inform the Contracting Party to whose jurisdiction the witness or other person is subject. The same provisions shall apply if a witness or expert has, in the opinion of the Chamber, violated the oath or solemn declaration provided for in Rule 66.

Rule 70

(Verbatim record of hearings)

1   The Registrar shall, if the Chamber so directs, be responsible for the making of a verbatim record of a hearing. The verbatim record shall include

a the composition of the Chamber at the hearing;

b   a list of those appearing before the Court, that is to say Agents, advocates and advisers of the parties and any third party taking part;

c   the surname, forename, description and address of each witness, expert or other person heard;

d   the text of statements made, questions put and replies given;

e   the text of any decision delivered during the hearing by the Chamber or the President of the Chamber.

2   If all or part of the verbatim record is in a non-official language, the Registrar shall, if the Chamber so directs, arrange for its translation into one of the official languages.

3   The representatives of the parties shall receive a copy of the verbatim record in order that they may, subject to the control of the Registrar or the President of the Chamber, make corrections, but in no case may such corrections affect the sense and bearing of what was said. The Registrar shall lay down, in accordance with the instructions of the President of the Chamber, the time-limits granted for this purpose.

4   The verbatim record, once so corrected, shall be signed by the President and the Registrar and shall then constitute certified matters of record.

Chapter VII – Proceedings before the Grand Chamber

Rule 71

(Applicability of procedural provisions)

Any provisions governing proceedings before the Chambers shall apply, mutatis mutandis, to proceedings before the Grand Chamber.

Rule 72

(Relinquishment of jurisdiction by a Chamber in favour of the Grand Chamber)

1   In accordance with Article 30 of the Convention, where a case pending before a Chamber raises a serious question affecting the interpretation of the Convention or the protocols thereto or where the resolution of a question before it might have a result inconsistent with a judgment previously delivered by the Court, the Chamber may, at any time before it has rendered its judgment, relinquish jurisdiction in favour of the Grand Chamber, unless one of the parties to the case has objected in accordance with paragraph 2 of this Rule. Reasons need not be given for the decision to relinquish.

2   The Registrar shall notify the parties of the Chamber's intention to relinquish jurisdiction. The parties shall have one month from the date of that notification within which to file at the Registry a duly reasoned objection. An objection which does not fulfil these conditions shall be considered invalid by the Chamber.

Rule 73

(Request by a party for referral of a case to the Grand Chamber)

1   In accordance with Article 43 of the Convention, any party to a case may exceptionally, within a period of three months from the date of delivery of the judgment of a Chamber, file in writing at the Registry a request that the case be referred to the Grand Chamber. The party shall specify in its request the serious question affecting the interpretation or application of the Convention or the protocols thereto, or the serious issue of general importance, which in its view warrants consideration by the Grand Chamber.

2   A panel of five judges of the Grand Chamber constituted in accordance with Rule 24 § 6 shall examine the request solely on the basis of the existing case file. It shall accept the request only if it considers that the case does raise such a question or issue. Reasons need not be given for a refusal of the request.

3   If the panel accepts the request, the Grand Chamber shall decide the case by means of a judgment.

Chapter VIII – Judgments

Rule 74

(Contents of the judgment)

1   A judgment as referred to in Articles 42 and 44 of the Convention shall contain

a the names of the President and the other judges constituting the Chamber concerned, and the name of the Registrar or the Deputy Registrar;

b the dates on which it was adopted and delivered;

c a description of the parties;

d the names of the Agents, advocates or advisers of the parties;

e an account of the procedure followed;

f the facts of the case;

g a summary of the submissions of the parties;

h the reasons in point of law;

i the operative provisions;

j the decision, if any, in respect of costs;

k the number of judges constituting the majority;

l where appropriate, a statement as to which text is authentic.

2 Any judge who has taken part in the consideration of the case shall be entitled to annex to the judgment either a separate opinion, concurring with or dissenting from that judgment, or a bare statement of dissent.

Rule 75

(Ruling on just satisfaction)

1 Where the Chamber finds that there has been a violation of the Convention, it shall give in the same judgment a ruling on the application of Article 41 of the Convention if that question, after being raised in accordance with Rule 60, is ready for decision; if the question is not ready for decision, the Chamber shall reserve it in whole or in part and shall fix the further procedure.

2 For the purposes of ruling on the application of Article 41 of the Convention, the Chamber shall, as far as possible, be composed of those judges who sat to consider the merits of the case. Where it is not possible to constitute the original Chamber, the President of the Court shall complete or compose the Chamber by drawing lots.

3 The Chamber may, when affording just satisfaction under Article 41 of the Convention, direct that if settlement is not made within a specified time, interest is to be payable on any sums awarded.

4 If the Court is informed that an agreement has been reached between the injured party and the Contracting Party liable, it shall verify the equitable nature of the agreement and, where it finds the agreement to be equitable, strike the case out of the list in accordance with Rule 44 § 2.

Rule 76

(Language of the judgment)

1   Unless the Court decides that a judgment shall be given in both official languages, all judgments shall be given either in English or in French. Judgments given shall be accessible to the public.

2   Publication of such judgments in the official reports of the Court, as provided for in Rule 78, shall be in both official languages of the Court.

Rule 77

(Signature, delivery and notification of the judgment)

1   Judgments shall be signed by the President of the Chamber and the Registrar.

2   The judgment may be read out at a public hearing by the President of the Chamber or by another judge delegated by him or her. The Agents and representatives of the parties shall be informed in due time of the date of the hearing. Otherwise the notification provided for in paragraph 3 of this Rule shall constitute delivery of the judgment.

3   The judgment shall be transmitted to the Committee of Ministers. The Registrar shall send certified copies to the parties, to the Secretary General of the Council of Europe, to any third party and to any other person directly concerned. The original copy, duly signed and sealed, shall be placed in the archives of the Court.

Rule 78

(Publication of judgments and other documents)

In accordance with Article 44 § 3 of the Convention, final judgments of the Court shall be published, under the responsibility of the Registrar, in an appropriate form. The Registrar shall in addition be responsible for the publication of official reports of selected judgments and decisions and of any document which the President of the Court considers it useful to publish.

Rule 79

(Request for interpretation of a judgment)

1   A party may request the interpretation of a judgment within a period of one year following the delivery of that judgment.

2   The request shall be filed with the Registry. It shall state precisely the point or points in the operative provisions of the judgment on which interpretation is required.

3   The original Chamber may decide of its own motion to refuse the request on the ground that there is no reason to warrant considering it. Where it is not possible to constitute the original Chamber, the President of the Court shall complete or compose the Chamber by drawing lots.

4   If the Chamber does not refuse the request, the Registrar shall communicate it to the other party or parties and shall invite them to submit any written comments within a time-limit laid down by the President of the Chamber. The President of the Chamber shall also fix the date of the hearing should the Chamber decide to hold one. The Chamber shall decide by means of a judgment.

Rule 80

(Request for revision of a judgment)

1   A party may, in the event of the discovery of a fact which might by its nature have a decisive influence and which, when a judgment was delivered, was unknown to the Court and could not reasonably have been known to that party, request the Court, within a period of six months after that party acquired knowledge of the fact, to revise that judgment.

2   The request shall mention the judgment of which revision is requested and shall contain the information necessary to show that the conditions laid down in paragraph 1 have been complied with. It shall be accompanied by a copy of all supporting documents. The request and supporting documents shall be filed with the Registry.

3   The original Chamber may decide of its own motion to refuse the request on the ground that there is no reason to warrant considering it. Where it is not possible to constitute the original Chamber, the President of the Court shall complete or compose the Chamber by drawing lots.

4   If the Chamber does not refuse the request, the Registrar shall communicate it to the other party or parties and shall invite them to submit any written comments within a time-limit laid down by the President of the Chamber. The President of the Chamber shall also fix the date of the hearing should the Chamber decide to hold one. The Chamber shall decide by means of a judgment.

Rule 81

(Rectification of errors in decisions and judgments)

Without prejudice to the provisions on revision of judgments and on restoration to the list of applications, the Court may, of its own motion or at the request of a party made within one month of the delivery of a decision or a judgment, rectify clerical errors, errors in calculation or obvious mistakes.

Chapter IX – Advisory Opinions

Rule 82

In proceedings relating to advisory opinions the Court shall apply, in addition to the provisions of Articles 47, 48 and 49 of the Convention, the provisions which follow. It shall also apply the other provisions of these Rules to the extent to which it considers this to be appropriate.

Rule 83

The request for an advisory opinion shall be filed with the Registry. It shall state fully and precisely the question on which the opinion of the Court is sought, and also

a the date on which the Committee of Ministers adopted the decision referred to in Article 47 § 3 of the Convention;

b the names and addresses of the person or persons appointed by the Committee of Ministers to give the Court any explanations which it may require.

The request shall be accompanied by all documents likely to elucidate the question.

Rule 84

1 On receipt of a request, the Registrar shall transmit a copy of it to all members of the Court.

2 The Registrar shall inform the Contracting Parties that the Court is prepared to receive their written comments.

Rule 85

1 The President of the Court shall lay down the time-limits for filing written comments or other documents.

2 Written comments or other documents shall be filed with the Registry. The Registrar shall transmit copies of them to all the members of the Court, to the Committee of Ministers and to each of the Contracting Parties.

Rule 86

After the close of the written procedure, the President of the Court shall decide whether the Contracting Parties which have submitted written comments are to be given an opportunity to develop them at an oral hearing held for the purpose.

Rule 87

If the Court considers that the request for an advisory opinion is not within its consultative competence as defined in Article 47 of the Convention, it shall so declare in a reasoned decision.

Rule 88

1   Advisory opinions shall be given by a majority vote of the Grand Chamber. They shall mention the number of judges constituting the majority.

2   Any judge may, if he or she so desires, attach to the opinion of the Court either a separate opinion, concurring with or dissenting from the advisory opinion, or a bare statement of dissent.

Rule 89

The advisory opinion shall be read out in one of the two official languages by the President of the Court, or by another judge delegated by the President, at a public hearing, prior notice having been given to the Committee of Ministers and to each of the Contracting Parties.

Rule 90

The opinion, or any decision given under Rule 87, shall be signed by the President of the Court and by the Registrar. The original copy, duly signed and sealed, shall be placed in the archives of the Court. The Registrar shall send certified copies to the Committee of Ministers, to the Contracting Parties and to the Secretary General of the Council of Europe.

Chapter X – Legal aid

Rule 91

1   The President of the Chamber may, either at the request of an applicant lodging an application under Article 34 of the Convention or of his or her own motion, grant free legal aid to the applicant in connection with the presentation of the case from the moment when observations in writing on the admissibility of that application are received from the respondent Contracting Party in accordance with Rule 54 § 3 (b), or where the time-limit for their submission has expired.

2   Subject to Rule 96, where the applicant has been granted legal aid in connection with the presentation of his or her case before the Chamber, that grant shall continue in force for purposes of his or her representation before the Grand Chamber.

Rule 92

Legal aid shall be granted only where the President of the Chamber is satisfied

a that it is necessary for the proper conduct of the case before the Chamber;

b that the applicant has insufficient means to meet all or part of the costs entailed.

Rule 93

1 In order to determine whether or not applicants have sufficient means to meet all or part of the costs entailed, they shall be required to complete a form of declaration stating their income, capital assets and any financial commitments in respect of dependants, or any other financial obligations. The declaration shall be certified by the appropriate domestic authority or authorities.

2 The Contracting Party concerned shall be requested to submit its comments in writing.

3 After receiving the information mentioned in paragraphs 1 and 2 above, the President of the Chamber shall decide whether or not to grant legal aid. The Registrar shall inform the parties accordingly.

Rule 94

1 Fees shall be payable to the advocates or other persons appointed in accordance with Rule 36 § 4. Fees may, where appropriate, be paid to more than one such representative.

2 Legal aid may be granted to cover not only representatives' fees but also travelling and subsistence expenses and other necessary expenses incurred by the applicant or appointed representative.

Rule 95

On a decision to grant legal aid, the Registrar shall

a fix the rate of fees to be paid in accordance with the legal-aid scales in force;

b the level of expenses to be paid.

Rule 96

The President of the Chamber may, if satisfied that the conditions stated in Rule 92 are no longer fulfilled, revoke or vary a grant of legal aid at any time.

Title III – Transitional rules

Rule 97

(Judges' terms of office)

The duration of the terms of office of the judges who were members of the Court at the date of the entry into force of Protocol No. 11 to the Convention shall be calculated as from that date.

Rule 98

(Presidency of the Sections)

For a period of three years from the entry into force of Protocol No. 11 to the Convention,

a the two Presidents of Sections who are not simultaneously Vice-Presidents of the Court and the Vice-Presidents of the Sections shall be elected for a term of office of eighteen months;

b the Vice-Presidents of the Sections may not be immediately re-elected.

Rule 99

(Relations between the Court and the Commission)

1 In cases brought before the Court under Article 5 §§ 4 and 5 of Protocol No. 11 to the Convention the Court may invite the Commission to delegate one or more of its members to take part in the consideration of the case before the Court.

2 In cases referred to in the preceding paragraph the Court shall take into consideration the report of the Commission adopted pursuant to former Article 31 of the Convention.

3 Unless the President of the Chamber decides otherwise, the said report shall be made available to the public through the Registrar as soon as possible after the case has been brought before the Court.

4 The remainder of the case file of the Commission, including all pleadings, in cases brought before the Court under Article 5 §§ 2 to 5 of Protocol No. 11 shall remain confidential unless the President of the Chamber decides otherwise.

5 In cases where the Commission has taken evidence but has been unable to adopt a report in accordance with former Article 31 of the Convention, the Court shall take into consideration the verbatim records, documentation and opinion of the Commission's delegations arising from such investigations.

Rule 100

(Chamber and Grand Chamber proceedings)

1   In cases referred to the Court under Article 5 § 4 of Protocol No. 11 to the Convention, a panel of the Grand Chamber constituted in accordance with Rule 24 § 6 shall determine, solely on the basis of the existing case file, whether a Chamber or the Grand Chamber is to decide the case.

2   If the case is decided by a Chamber, the judgment of the Chamber shall, in accordance with Article 5 § 4 of Protocol No. 11, be final and Rule 73 shall be inapplicable.

3   Cases transmitted to the Court under Article 5 § 5 of Protocol No. 11 shall be forwarded by the President of the Court to the Grand Chamber.

4   For each case transmitted to the Grand Chamber under Article 5 § 5 of the Protocol No 11, the Grand Chamber shall be completed by judges designated by rotation within one of the groups mentioned in Rule 24 § 3, the cases being allocated to the groups on an alternate basis.

Rule 101

(Grant of legal aid)

Subject to Rule 96, in cases brought before the Court under Article 5 §§ 2 to 5 of Protocol No. 11 to the Convention, a grant of legal aid made to an applicant in the proceedings before the Commission or the former Court shall continue in force for the purposes of his or her representation before the Court.

Rule 102

(Request for interpretation or revision of a judgment)

1   Where a party requests interpretation or revision of a judgment delivered by the former Court, the President of the Court shall assign the request to one of the Sections in accordance with the conditions laid down in Rule 51 or 52, as the case may be.

2   The President of the relevant Section shall, notwithstanding Rules 79 § 3 and 80 § 3, constitute a new Chamber to consider the request.

3   The Chamber to be constituted shall include as ex officio members

    a the President of the Section;

and, whether or not they are members of the relevant Section,

    b the judge elected in respect of any Contracting Party concerned or, if he or she is unable to sit, any judge appointed under Rule 29;

    c any judge of the Court who was a member of the original Chamber that delivered the judgment in the former Court.

4   a   The other members of the Chamber shall be designated by the President of the Section by means of a drawing of lots from among the members of the relevant Section.

b The members of the Section who are not so designated shall sit in the case as substitute judges.

Title IV – Final clauses

Rule 103

(Amendment or suspension of a Rule)

1   Any Rule may be amended upon a motion made after notice where such a motion is carried at the next session of the plenary Court by a majority of all the members of the Court. Notice of such a motion shall be delivered in writing to the Registrar at least one month before the session at which it is to be discussed. On receipt of such a notice of motion, the Registrar shall inform all members of the Court at the earliest possible moment.

2   A Rule relating to the internal working of the Court may be suspended upon a motion made without notice, provided that this decision is taken unanimously by the Chamber concerned. The suspension of a Rule shall in this case be limited in its operation to the particular purpose for which it was sought.

Rule 104

(Entry into force of the Rules)

The present Rules shall enter into force on 1 November 1998.

European Agreement relating to Persons Participating in Proceedings of the European Court of Human Rights
(European Treaty Series, No. 161)

Strasbourg, 5.III.1996

The member States of the Council of Europe, signatories hereto,

Having regard to the Convention for the Protection of Human Rights and Fundamental Freedoms, signed at Rome on 4 November 1950 (hereinafter referred to as "the Convention");

Recalling the European Agreement relating to Persons Participating in Proceedings of the European Commission and Court of Human Rights, signed at London on 6 May 1969;

Having regard to Protocol No. 11 to the Convention, restructuring the control machinery established thereby, signed at Strasbourg on 11 May 1994 (hereinafter referred to as "Protocol No. 11 to the Convention"), which establishes a permanent European Court of Human Rights (hereinafter referred to as "the Court") to replace the European Commission and Court of Human Rights;

Considering, in the light of this development, that it is advisable for the better fulfilment of the purposes of the Convention that persons taking part in proceedings before the Court be accorded certain immunities and facilities by a new Agreement, the European Agreement relating to Persons Participating in Proceedings of the European Court of Human Rights (hereinafter referred to as "this Agreement"),

Have agreed as follows:

Article 1

1 The persons to whom this Agreement applies are:
   a any persons taking part in proceedings instituted before the Court as parties, their representatives and advisers;
   b witnesses and experts called upon by the Court and other persons invited by the President of the Court to take part in proceedings.

2 For the purposes of this Agreement, the term "Court" shall include committees, chambers, a panel of the Grand Chamber, the Grand Chamber and the judges. The term "taking part in proceedings" shall include

making communications with a view to a complaint against a State Party to the Convention.

3   If in the course of the exercise by the Committee of Ministers of its functions under Article 46, paragraph 2, of the Convention, any person mentioned in paragraph 1 above is called upon to appear before, or to submit written statements to the Committee of Ministers, the provisions of this Agreement shall apply in relation to him.

Article 2

1   The persons referred to in paragraph 1 of Article 1 of this Agreement shall have immunity from legal process in respect of oral or written statements made, or documents or other evidence submitted by them before or to the Court.

2   This immunity does not apply to communication outside the Court of any such statements, documents or evidence submitted to the Court.

Article 3

1   The Contracting Parties shall respect the right of the persons referred to in paragraph 1 of Article 1 of this Agreement to correspond freely with the Court.

2   As regards persons under detention, the exercise of this right shall in particular imply that:

a   their correspondence shall be despatched and delivered without undue delay and without alteration;

b   such persons shall not be subject to disciplinary measures in any form on account of any communication sent through the proper channels to the Court;

c   such persons shall have the right to correspond, and consult out of hearing of other persons, with a lawyer qualified to appear before the courts of the country where they are detained in regard to an application to the Court, or any proceedings resulting therefrom.

3   In application of the preceding paragraphs, there shall be no interference by a public authority except such as is in accordance with the law and is necessary in a democratic society in the interests of national security, for the detection or prosecution of a criminal offence or for the protection of health.

Article 4

1   a   The Contracting Parties undertake not to hinder the free movement and travel, for the purpose of attending and returning from proceedings before the Court, of persons referred to in paragraph 1 of Arti-

cle 1 of this Agreement.

b   No restrictions shall be placed on their movement and travel other than such as are in accordance with the law and necessary in a democratic society in the interests of national security or public safety, for the maintenance of *ordre public*, for the prevention of crime, for the protection of health or morals, or for the protection of the rights and freedoms of others.

2   a   Such persons shall not, in countries of transit and in the country where the proceedings take place, be prosecuted or detained or be subjected to any other restriction of their personal liberty in respect of acts or convictions prior to the commencement of the journey.

b   Any Contracting Party may, at the time of signature, ratification, acceptance or approval of this Agreement, declare that the provisions of this paragraph will not apply to its own nationals. Such a declaration may be withdrawn at any time by means of a notification addressed to the Secretary General of the Council of Europe.

3   The Contracting Parties undertake to re-admit on his return to their territory any such person who commenced his journey in the said territory.

4   The provisions of paragraphs 1 and 2 of this Article shall cease to apply when the person concerned has had, for a period of fifteen consecutive days from the date when his presence is no longer required by the Court, the opportunity of returning to the country from which his journey commenced.

5   Where there is any conflict between the obligations of a Contracting Party resulting from paragraph 2 of this Article and those resulting from a Council of Europe convention or from an extradition treaty or other treaty concerning mutual assistance in criminal matters with other Contracting Parties, the provisions of paragraph 2 of this Article shall prevail.

Article 5

1   Immunities and facilities are accorded to the persons referred to in paragraph 1 of Article 1 of this Agreement solely in order to ensure for them the freedom of speech and the independence necessary for the discharge of their functions, tasks or duties, or the exercise of their rights in relation to the Court.

2   a   The Court shall alone be competent to waive, in whole or in part, the immunity provided for in paragraph 1 of Article 2 of this Agreement; it has not only the right but the duty to waive immunity in any case where, in its opinion, such immunity would impede the course of justice and waiver in whole or in part would not prejudice the purpose defined in paragraph 1 of this article.

b The immunity may be waived by the Court, either *ex officio* or at the request of any Contracting Party or of any person concerned.

c Decisions waiving immunity or refusing the waiver shall be accompanied by a statement of reasons.

3 If a Contracting Party certifies that waiver of the immunity provided for in paragraph 1 of Article 2 of this Agreement is necessary for the purpose of proceedings in respect of an offence against national security, the Court shall waive immunity to the extent specified in the certificate.

4 In the event of the discovery of a fact which might, by its nature, have a decisive influence and which at the time of the decision refusing waiver of immunity was unknown to the author of the request, the latter may make a new request to the Court.

Article 6

Nothing in this Agreement shall be construed as limiting or derogating from any of the obligations assumed by the Contracting Parties under the Convention or its protocols.

Article 7

1 This Agreement shall be open for signature by the member States of the Council of Europe, which may express their consent to be bound by:

a signature without reservation as to ratification, acceptance or approval; or

b signature, subject to ratification, acceptance or approval, followed by ratification, acceptance or approval.

2 Instruments of ratification, acceptance or approval shall be deposited with the Secretary General of the Council of Europe.

Article 8

1 This Agreement shall enter into force on the first day of the month following the expiration of a period of one month after the date on which ten member States of the Council of Europe have expressed their consent to be bound by the Agreement in accordance with the provisions of Article 7 or on the date of entry into force of Protocol No. 11 to the Convention, whichever is the later.

2 In respect of any member State which subsequently expresses its consent to be bound by it, this Agreement shall enter into force on the first day of the month following the expiration of a period of one month after the date of such signature or of the deposit of the instrument of ratification, acceptance or approval.

Article 9

1 Any Contracting State may, when depositing its instrument of ratification, acceptance or approval or at any later date, by declaration addressed to the Secretary General of the Council of Europe, extend this Agreement to any territory or territories specified in the declaration and for whose international relations it is responsible or on whose behalf it is authorised to give undertakings.

2 This Agreement shall enter into force for any territory or territories specified in a declaration made pursuant to paragraph 1 on the first day of the month following the expiration of one month after the date of receipt of the declaration by the Secretary General.

3 Any declaration made pursuant to paragraph 1 may, in respect of any territory mentioned in such declaration, be withdrawn according to the procedure laid down for denunciation in Article 10 of this Agreement.

Article 10

1 This Agreement shall remain in force indefinitely.

2 Any Contracting Party may, insofar as it is concerned, denounce this Agreement by means of a notification addressed to the Secretary General of the Council of Europe.

3 Such denunciation shall take effect six months after the date of receipt by the Secretary General of such notification. Such denunciation shall not have the effect of releasing the Contracting Parties concerned from any obligation which may have arisen under this Agreement in relation to any person referred to in paragraph 1 of Article 1.

Article 11

The Secretary General of the Council of Europe shall notify the member States of the Council of:

a any signature;

b the deposit of any instrument of ratification, acceptance or approval;

c any date of entry into force of this Agreement in accordance with Articles 8 and 9 thereof;

d any other act, notification or communication relating to this Agreement.

In witness whereof the undersigned, being duly authorised thereto, have signed this Agreement.

Done at Strasbourg, this 5th day of March 1996, in English and French, both texts being equally authentic, in a single copy which shall be deposited in the archives of the Council of Europe. The Secretary General of the Council of Europe shall transmit certified copies to each member State of the Council of Europe.

Rules adopted by the Committee of Ministers for the application of Articles 32 and 54 of the European Convention on Human Rights[1]

Article 32

Text approved by the Committee of Ministers at the 181st meeting of the Ministers' Deputies in June 1969[2] and amended at the 215th (November 1972), 245th (May 1975), 307th (September 1979), 409th (June 1987), 449th (December 1990) and 451st (January 1991) meetings and at the special meeting of the Ministers' Deputies on 19 December 1991.

A Rules of substance

Rule 1

When exercising its functions under Article 32 of the Convention, the Committee of Ministers is entitled to discuss the substance of any case on which the Commission has submitted a report, for example by considering written or oral statements of the parties and hearing of witnesses (see Rule 4).

Rule 2

The representative of any member state on the Committee of Ministers shall be fully qualified to take part in exercising the functions and powers set forth in Article 32 of the Convention, even if that state has not yet ratified the Convention.

Rule 3

Each representative on the Committee of Ministers has an instrinsic right to make submissions and deposit documents. Consequently, the representative on the Committee of Ministers of a government which was not a party to the proceedings before the Commission, may play a full part in the proceedings before the Committee of Ministers.[3]

---

1. The article numbers in this section refer to those of the Convention prior to the entry into force of Protocol No. 11. At the time this volume was prepared the Committee of Ministers had not adopted new rules to take account of the provisions of the Convention as amended.
2. The text approved at the 181st meeting of the Ministers' Deputies contained a restatement of the rules previously adopted at the 68th (January 1959), 94th (January 1961), 99th (May 1961), 140th (April 1965) and 164th (October 1967) meetings.
3. See Appendix, p. 116, paragraph 1.

Rule 4

While the Committee of Ministers must have all the necessary powers to reach a decision on a report of the Commission, nevertheless, it may not itself wish to undertake the task of taking evidence, etc., should the need arise. The procedure to be followed in such a case will be decided *ad hoc*.[1]

Rule 5[2]

Rule 6

The Committee of Ministers considers that the Commission is not entitled to make proposals under Article 31, paragraph 3, of the Convention in cases where it considers that there has not been a violation of the Convention.

Rule 6 bis

Prior to taking a decision under Article 32, paragraph 1, of the Convention, the Committee of Ministers may be informed of a friendly settlement, arrangement or other fact of a kind to provide a solution of the matter. In that event, it may decide to discontinue its examination of the case, after satisfying itself that the solution envisaged is based on respect for human rights as defined in the Convention.

B Procedural rules

Rule 7

If the chairmanship of the Committee of Ministers is held by the representative of a state which is party to a dispute referred to the Committee of Ministers, that representative shall step down from the chair during the discussion of the Commission's report.

Rule 8

The Chairman of the Committee shall obtain the opinion of the representatives of the State Party or States Parties to the dispute in regard to the procedure to be followed, and the Committee shall specify, if necessary, in what order and within what time-limits any written submissions or other documents are to be deposited.[3]

Rule 9

1   During the examination of the case and before taking the decision mentioned in Article 32, paragraph 1, of the Convention, the Committee of Min-

---

1. See Appendix, p. 116, paragraph 2.
2. Rule 5 was deleted by the Ministers' Deputies on 19 December 1991.
3. This Rule applies not only to inter-state disputes but also when the Committee of Ministers is considering the report of the Commission on an individual application.

isters may, if it deems advisable, request the Commission for information on particular points in the report which it has transmitted to the Committee.

2   After taking a decision under Article 32, paragraph 1, to the effect that there has been a violation of the Convention, the Committee of Ministers may request the Commission to make proposals concerning in particular the appropriateness, nature and extent of just satisfaction for the injured party.

Rule 9 bis

When a vote is taken in accordance with Article 32, paragraph 1, and the majority required to decide whether there has been a violation of the Convention has not been attained, a second and final vote shall be taken at one of the three following meetings of the Committee of Ministers.

Rule 9 ter

1   The Commission's report shall be published when the Committee of Ministers has completed consideration of the case under Article 32, paragraph 1.

2   The Committee of Ministers may, by way of exception and without prejudice to Article 32, paragraph 3, decide not to publish a report of the Commission or a part thereof upon a reasoned request of a Contracting Party or of the Commission.

Rule 10

In the matter of voting, the rules laid down in Article 20 of the Statute should, in general, apply.[1] In particular:

a   the parties to the dispute shall have the right to vote;

b   decisions taken in pursuance of Rule 6 bis require a two-thirds majority of the representatives casting a vote and a majority of the representatives entitled to sit on the Committee;

c   certain questions of procedure, such as in what order and within what time-limits any written submissions or other documents are to be deposited, shall be determined by a simple majority of the representatives entitled to sit on the Committee.

---

1. In the case of a decision by the Committee of Ministers on the question whether there has been a violation of the Convention, paragraph 1 of Article 32 of the Convention already provides that "the Committee of Ministers shall decide by a majority of two-thirds of the members entitled to sit on the Committee whether there has been a violation of the Convention".

Rule 11

The decision taken under Article 32, paragraph 1, will be published in the form of a resolution adopted by a two-thirds majority of the representatives casting a vote and a majority of the representatives entitled to sit on the Committee.

Appendix – Other points discussed by the Committee of Ministers

1   With reference to Rule 3 above, the Committee of Ministers reserved its position on the possibility that the representative of a government which had not been a party to the proceedings before the Commission might make a request to the Committee of Ministers which had not been made before the Commission (for example, a request for damages).

2   In connection with Rule 4, the Committee of Ministers considered that while it must have all the necessary powers to reach a decision on a case submitted to it, nevertheless it is not well-equipped to take evidence, etc. and ought not normally to undertake such tasks. If therefore it should become necessary for the Committee of Ministers to take evidence, etc. when it is considering a case under Article 32, there are the following possibilities:

a   to conclude a Protocol to the Convention conferring on the Commission the power to undertake such tasks on behalf of the Committee of Ministers;

b   to invite the Commission to undertake these tasks on its behalf, since the Commission is in its nature better equipped to do so, if the Commission agrees to this procedure;

c   the Committee of Ministers could take evidence, etc. in plenary sessions (possibly with alternate members) or appoint a sub-committee for the purpose;

d   under Article 17 of the Statute, the Committee of Ministers may set up advisory and technical committees for specific purposes.

The Committee of Ministers decided not to adopt the first of these possibilities but to leave the choice open for a decision ad hoc should the need arise.

2 *bis*   The Committee of Ministers decided that in every case in which it finds there has been a violation of the Convention, it would consider, taking into account any proposals from the Commission, whether just satisfaction should be afforded to the injured party and, if necessary, indicate measures on this subject to the state concerned.

3   a   The Committee of Ministers decided not to establish a procedure permitting the communication to an applicant of the report of the Commission on his application, or the communication to the Committee of Ministers of the applicant's observations on the report.

b The communication to an individual applicant of the complete text or extracts from the report of the Commission should take place only as an exceptional measure (for example, where the Committee of Ministers wishes to obtain the observations of the applicant), only on a strictly confidential basis, and only with the consent of the state against which the application was lodged.

c Since the individual applicant is not a party to the proceedings before the Committee of Ministers under Article 32 of the Convention, he has no right to be heard by the Committee of Ministers or to have any written communication considered by the Committee.

This should be explained by the Secretary General to the applicant when he writes to inform him that the report of the Commission on his case has been transmitted to the Committee of Ministers in accordance with the provisions of Article 31 of the Convention.

d If communications from the individual applicant intended for the Committee of Ministers are nevertheless received, the Secretary General should acknowledge their receipt and explain to the applicant why they will not form part of the proceedings before the Committee of Ministers and cannot be considered as a document in the case. In appropriate cases, the Secretary General might add that it is possible for the applicant to submit a new application to the Commission if he wishes to invoke important new information.

4 The Committee of Ministers decided not to make provisions in its Rules for participation by delegates of the Commission in its proceedings, since the Commission considered that such participation would be outside its powers as defined in the Convention.[1]

The Committee of Ministers at the 307th meeting of the Ministers' Deputies (September 1979) adopted the following additional Rules:

a An individual applicant ought normally to be informed of the outcome of the examination of his case before the Committee of Ministers. It would be for the Committee of Ministers to decide in each particular case on the information to be communicated and on the procedure to be followed;

---

1. At the 245th meeting of the Ministers' Deputies (May 1975), the Deputies agreed, unless otherwise decided in a particular case, to transmit to the European Commission of Human Rights, at the end of their discussions on a case referred to the Committee of Ministers in accordance with Article 32 of the European Convention on Human Rights, the texts of every decision appearing in their conclusions, on the understanding that these texts are not made public; they agreed also that this decision cannot be regarded as a precedent with regard to other decisions of the Committee.

b a decision to inform an individual applicant about the outcome of his case should be taken, in accordance with Article 21 b of the Statute, by unanimous vote;

c the Committee of Ministers could indicate in its communication to the applicant if any of the information conveyed to him is to be treated as confidential.

Article 54

Text approved by the Committee of Ministers at the 254th Meeting of the Ministers' Deputies in February 1976.

Rule 1

When a judgment of the Court is transmitted to the Committee of Ministers in accordance with Article 54 of the Convention, the case shall be inscribed on the agenda of the Committee without delay.

Rule 2

a When, in the judgment transmitted to the Committee of Ministers in accordance with Article 54 of the Convention, the Court decides that there has been a violation of the Convention and/or affords just satisfaction to the injured party under Article 50 of the Convention, the Committee shall invite the state concerned to inform it of the measures which it has taken in consequence of the judgment, having regard to its obligation under Article 53 of the Convention to abide by the judgment.[1]

b If the state concerned informs the Committee of Ministers that it is not yet in a position to inform it of the measures taken, the case shall be automatically inscribed on the agenda of a meeting of the Committee taking place not more than six months later, unless the Committee of Ministers decides otherwise; the same Rule will be applied on expiration of this and any subsequent period.

Rule 3

The Committee of Ministers shall not regard its functions under Article 54 of the Convention as having been exercised until it has taken note of the information supplied in accordance with Rule 2 and, when just satisfaction has

---

1. At the 215th meeting of the Ministers' Deputies (November 1972), it was agreed that the Committee of Ministers is entitled to consider a communication from an individual who claims that he has not received damages in accordance with a decision of the Court under Article 50 of the Convention affording him just satisfaction as an injured party, as well as any further information furnished to it concerning the execution of such a judgment of the Court, and that, consequently, any such communication should be distributed to the Committee of Ministers.

been afforded, until it has satisfied itself that the state concerned has awarded this just satisfaction to the injured party.

Rule 4

The decision in which the Committee of Ministers declares that its functions under

Article 54 of the Convention have been exercised shall take the form of a resolution.

European Convention on Human Rights and protocols: signatures and ratifications at 1 January 1999

Member state	ECHR		Protocol No. 1		Protocol No. 4		Protocol No. 6		Protocol No. 7	
	Signed	Ratified	Signed	Ratified	Signed	Ratified	Signed	Ratified	Signed	Ratified
Albania	13/07/95	02/10/96	02/10/96	02/10/96	02/10/96	02/10/96	–	–	02/10/96	02/10/96
Andorra	10/11/94	22/01/96	–	–	–	–	22/01/96	22/01/96	–	–
Austria	13/12/57	03/09/58	13/12/57	03/09/58	16/09/63	18/09/69	28/04/83	05/01/84	19/03/85	14/05/86
Belgium	04/11/50	14/06/55	20/03/52	14/06/55	16/09/63	21/09/70	28/04/83	10/12/98	–	–
Bulgaria	07/05/92	07/09/92	07/05/92	07/09/92	03/11/93	–	–	–	03/11/93	–
Croatia	06/11/96	05/11/97	06/11/96	05/11/97	06/11/96	05/11/97	06/11/96	05/11/97	06/11/96	05/11/97
Cyprus	16/12/61	06/10/62	16/12/61	06/10/62	06/10/88	03/10/89	–	–	–	–
Czech Republic*	21/02/91	18/03/92	21/02/91	18/03/92	21/02/91	18/03/92	21/02/91	18/03/92	21/02/91	18/03/92
Denmark	04/11/50	13/04/53	20/03/52	13/04/53	16/09/63	30/09/64	28/04/83	01/12/83	22/11/84	18/08/88
Estonia	14/05/93	16/04/96	14/05/93	16/04/96	14/05/93	16/04/96	14/05/93	17/04/98	14/05/93	16/04/96
Finland	05/05/89	10/05/90	05/05/89	10/05/90	05/05/89	10/05/90	05/05/89	10/05/90	05/05/89	10/05/90
France	04/11/50	03/05/74	20/03/52	03/05/74	22/10/73	03/05/74	28/04/83	17/02/86	22/11/84	17/02/86
Germany	04/11/50	05/12/52	20/03/52	13/02/57	16/09/63	01/06/68	28/04/83	05/07/89	19/03/85	–
Greece	28/11/50	28/11/74	20/03/52	28/11/74	–	–	02/05/83	08/09/98	22/11/84	29/10/87
Hungary	06/11/90	05/11/92	06/11/92	05/11/92	06/11/90	05/11/92	06/11/90	05/11/92	06/11/90	05/11/92
Iceland	04/11/50	29/06/53	20/03/52	29/06/53	16/11/67	16/11/67	24/04/85	22/05/87	19/03/85	22/05/87
Ireland	04/11/50	25/02/53	20/03/52	25/02/53	16/09/63	29/10/68	24/06/94	24/06/94	11/12/84	–
Italy	04/11/50	26/10/55	20/03/52	26/10/55	16/09/63	27/05/82	21/10/83	29/12/88	22/11/84	07/11/91
Latvia	10/02/95	27/06/97	21/03/97	27/06/97	21/03/97	27/06/97	26/06/98	–	21/03/97	27/06/97
Liechtenstein	23/11/78	08/09/82	07/05/87	14/11/95	–	–	15/11/90	15/11/90	–	–
Lithuania	14/05/93	20/06/95	14/05/93	24/05/96	14/05/93	20/06/95	–	–	14/05/93	20/06/95

Luxembourg	04/11/50	03/09/53	20/03/52	03/09/53	16/09/63	02/05/68	28/04/83	19/02/85	22/11/84	19/04/89
Malta	12/12/66	23/01/67	12/12/66	23/01/67	—	—	26/03/91	26/03/91	—	—
Moldova	13/07/95	12/09/97	02/05/96	12/09/97	02/05/96	12/09/97	02/05/96	12/09/97	02/05/96	12/09/97
Netherlands	04/11/50	31/08/54	20/03/52	31/08/54	15/11/63	23/06/82	28/04/83	25/04/86	22/11/84	—
Norway	04/11/50	15/01/52	20/03/52	18/12/52	16/09/63	12/06/64	28/04/83	25/10/88	22/11/84	25/10/88
Poland	26/11/91	19/01/93	14/09/92	10/10/94	14/09/92	10/10/94	—	—	14/09/92	—
Portugal	22/09/76	09/11/78	22/09/76	09/11/78	27/04/78	09/11/78	28/04/83	02/10/86	22/11/84	—
Romania	07/10/93	20/06/94	04/11/93	20/06/94	04/11/93	20/06/94	15/12/93	20/06/94	04/11/93	20/06/94
Russian Federation	28/02/96	05/05/98	28/02/96	05/05/98	28/02/96	05/05/98	16/04/97	—	28/02/96	05/05/98
San Marino	16/11/88	22/03/89	01/03/89	22/03/89	01/03/89	22/03/89	01/03/89	22/03/89	01/03/89	22/03/89
Slovakia*	21/02/91	18/03/92	21/02/91	18/03/92	21/02/91	18/03/92	21/02/91	18/03/92	21/02/91	18/03/92
Slovenia	14/05/93	28/06/94	14/05/93	28/06/94	14/05/93	28/06/94	14/05/93	28/06/94	14/05/93	28/06/94
Spain	24/11/77	04/10/79	23/02/78	27/11/90	23/02/78	—	28/04/83	14/01/85	22/11/84	—
Sweden	28/11/50	04/02/52	20/03/52	22/06/53	16/09/63	13/06/64	28/04/83	09/02/84	22/11/84	08/11/85
Switzerland	21/12/72	28/11/74	19/05/76	—	—	—	28/04/83	13/10/87	28/02/86	24/02/88
"The former Yugoslav Republic of Macedonia"	09/11/95	10/04/97	14/06/96	10/04/97	14/06/96	10/04/97	14/06/96	10/04/97	14/06/96	10/04/97
Turkey	04/11/50	18/05/54	20/03/52	18/05/54	19/10/92	—	—	—	14/03/85	—
Ukraine	09/11/95	11/09/97	19/12/96	11/09/97	19/12/96	11/09/97	05/05/97	—	19/12/96	11/09/97
United Kingdom	04/11/50	08/03/51	20/03/52	03/11/52	16/09/63	—	—	—	—	—

* Date of signature/deposit of the instrument of ratification by the Czech and Slovak Federal Republic.

European Convention
for the Prevention of Torture
and Inhuman or Degrading
Treatment or Punishment

and related texts

European Convention for the Prevention of Torture and Inhuman or Degrading Treatment or Punishment
(European Treaty Series, No. 126)

Strasbourg, 26.XI.1987

The member States of the Council of Europe, signatory hereto,

Having regard to the provisions of the Convention for the Protection of Human Rights and Fundamental Freedoms;

Recalling that, under Article 3 of the same Convention, "no one shall be subjected to torture or to inhuman or degrading treatment or punishment";

Noting that the machinery provided for in that Convention operates in relation to persons who allege that they are victims of violations of Article 3;

Convinced that the protection of persons deprived of their liberty against torture and inhuman or degrading treatment or punishment could be strengthened by non-judicial means of a preventive character based on visits,

Have agreed as follows:

Chapter I

Article 1

There shall be established a European Committee for the Prevention of Torture and Inhuman or Degrading Treatment or Punishment (hereinafter referred to as "the Committee"). The Committee shall, by means of visits, examine the treatment of persons deprived of their liberty with a view to strengthening, if necessary, the protection of such persons from torture and from inhuman or degrading treatment or punishment.

Article 2

Each Party shall permit visits, in accordance with this Convention, to any place within its jurisdiction where persons are deprived of their liberty by a public authority.

Article 3

In the application of this Convention, the Committee and the competent national authorities of the Party concerned shall co-operate with each other.

Chapter II

Article 4

1　The Committee shall consist of a number of members equal to that of the Parties.

2　The members of the Committee shall be chosen from among persons of high moral character, known for their competence in the field of human rights or having professional experience in the areas covered by this Convention.

3　No two members of the Committee may be nationals of the same State.

4　The members shall serve in their individual capacity, shall be independent and impartial, and shall be available to serve the Committee effectively.

Article 5

1　The members of the Committee shall be elected by the Committee of Ministers of the Council of Europe by an absolute majority of votes, from a list of names drawn up by the Bureau of the Consultative Assembly of the Council of Europe; each national delegation of the Parties in the Consultative Assembly shall put forward three candidates, of whom two at least shall be its nationals.

2　The same procedure shall be followed in filling casual vacancies.

3　The members of the Committee shall be elected for a period of four years. They may only be re-elected once. However, among the members elected at the first election, the terms of three members shall expire at the end of two years. The members whose terms are to expire at the end of the initial period of two years shall be chosen by lot by the Secretary General of the Council of Europe immediately after the first election has been completed.

Article 6

1　The Committee shall meet in camera. A quorum shall be equal to the majority of its members. The decisions of the Committee shall be taken by a majority of the members present, subject to the provisions of Article 10, paragraph 2.

2　The Committee shall draw up its own rules of procedure.

3   The Secretariat of the Committee shall be provided by the Secretary General of the Council of Europe.

Chapter III

Article 7

1   The Committee shall organise visits to places referred to in Article 2. Apart from periodic visits, the Committee may organise such other visits as appear to it to be required in the circumstances.

2   As a general rule, the visits shall be carried out by at least two members of the Committee. The Committee may, if it considers it necessary, be assisted by experts and interpreters.

Article 8

1   The Committee shall notify the Government of the Party concerned of its intention to carry out a visit. After such notification, it may at any time visit any place referred to in Article 2.

2   A Party shall provide the Committee with the following facilities to carry out its task:
    a   access to its territory and the right to travel without restriction;
    b   full information on the places where persons deprived of their liberty are being held;
    c   unlimited access to any place where persons are deprived of their liberty, including the right to move inside such places without restriction;
    d   other information available to the Party which is necessary for the Committee to carry out its task. In seeking such information, the Committee shall have regard to applicable rules of national law and professional ethics.

3   The Committee may interview in private persons deprived of their liberty.

4   The Committee may communicate freely with any person whom it believes can supply relevant information.

5   If necessary, the Committee may immediately communicate observations to the competent authorities of the Party concerned.

Article 9

1   In exceptional circumstances, the competent authorities of the Party concerned may make representations to the Committee against a visit at the time or to the particular place proposed by the Committee. Such representations may only be made on grounds of national defence, public safety, serious disorder in places where persons are deprived of their liberty,

the medical condition of a person or that an urgent interrogation relating to a serious crime is in progress.

2 Following such representations, the Committee and the Party shall immediately enter into consultations in order to clarify the situation and seek agreement on arrangements to enable the Committee to exercise its functions expeditiously. Such arrangements may include the transfer to another place of any person whom the Committee proposed to visit. Until the visit takes place, the Party shall provide information to the Committee about any person concerned.

Article 10

1 After each visit, the Committee shall draw up a report on the facts found during the visit, taking account of any observations which may have been submitted by the Party concerned. It shall transmit to the latter its report containing any recommendations it considers necessary. The Committee may consult with the Party with a view to suggesting, if necessary, improvements in the protection of persons deprived of their liberty.

2 If the Party fails to co-operate or refuses to improve the situation in the light of the Committee's recommendations, the Committee may decide, after the Party has had an opportunity to make known its views, by a majority of two-thirds of its members to make a public statement on the matter.

Article 11

1 The information gathered by the Committee in relation to a visit, its report and its consultations with the Party concerned shall be confidential.

2 The Committee shall publish its report, together with any comments of the Party concerned, whenever requested to do so by that Party.

3 However, no personal data shall be published without the express consent of the person concerned.

Article 12

Subject to the rules of confidentiality in Article 11, the Committee shall every year submit to the Committee of Ministers a general report on its activities which shall be transmitted to the Consultative Assembly and made public.

Article 13

The members of the Committee, experts and other persons assisting the Committee are required, during and after their terms of office, to maintain the confidentiality of the facts or information of which they have become aware during the discharge of their functions.

Article 14

1   The names of persons assisting the Committee shall be specified in the notification under Article 8, paragraph 1.

2   Experts shall act on the instructions and under the authority of the Committee. They shall have particular knowledge and experience in the areas covered by this Convention and shall be bound by the same duties of independence, impartiality and availability as the members of the Committee.

3   A Party may exceptionally declare that an expert or other person assisting the Committee may not be allowed to take part in a visit to a place within its jurisdiction.

Chapter IV

Article 15

Each Party shall inform the Committee of the name and address of the authority competent to receive notifications to its Government, and of any liaison officer it may appoint.

Article 16

The Committee, its members and experts referred to in Article 7, paragraph 2 shall enjoy the privileges and immunities set out in the Annex to this Convention.

Article 17

1   This Convention shall not prejudice the provisions of domestic law or any international agreement which provide greater protection for persons deprived of their liberty.

2   Nothing in this Convention shall be construed as limiting or derogating from the competence of the organs of the European Convention on Human Rights or from the obligations assumed by the Parties under that Convention.

3   The Committee shall not visit places which representatives or delegates of Protecting Powers or the International Committee of the Red Cross effectively visit on a regular basis by virtue of the Geneva Conventions of 12 August 1949 and the Additional Protocols of 8 June 1977 thereto.

Chapter V

Article 18

This Convention shall be open for signature by the member States of the Council of Europe. It is subject to ratification, acceptance or approval. Instruments of ratification, acceptance or approval shall be deposited with the Secretary General of the Council of Europe.

Article 19

1 This Convention shall enter into force on the first day of the month following the expiration of a period of three months after the date on which seven member States of the Council of Europe have expressed their consent to be bound by the Convention in accordance with the provisions of Article 18.

2 In respect of any member State which subsequently expresses its consent to be bound by it, the Convention shall enter into force on the first day of the month following the expiration of a period of three months after the date of the deposit of the instrument of ratification, acceptance or approval.

Article 20

1 Any State may at the time of signature or when depositing its instrument of ratification, acceptance or approval, specify the territory or territories to which this Convention shall apply.

2 Any State may at any later date, by a declaration addressed to the Secretary General of the Council of Europe, extend the application of this Convention to any other territory specified in the declaration. In respect of such territory the Convention shall enter into force on the first day of the month following the expiration of a period of three months after the date of receipt of such declaration by the Secretary General.

3 Any declaration made under the two preceding paragraphs may, in respect of any territory specified in such declaration, be withdrawn by a notification addressed to the Secretary General. The withdrawal shall become effective on the first day of the month following the expiration of a period of three months after the date of receipt of such notification by the Secretary General.

Article 21

No reservation may be made in respect of the provisions of this Convention.

Article 22

1 Any Party may, at any time, denounce this Convention by means of a notification addressed to the Secretary General of the Council of Europe.

2 Such denunciation shall become effective on the first day of the month following the expiration of a period of twelve months after the date of receipt of the notification by the Secretary General.

Article 23

The Secretary General of the Council of Europe shall notify the member States of the Council of Europe of:

a any signature;

b the deposit of any instrument of ratification, acceptance or approval;

c any date of entry into force of this Convention in accordance with Articles 19 and 20;

d any other act, notification or communication relating to this Convention, except for action taken in pursuance of Articles 8 and 10.

In witness whereof, the undersigned, being duly authorised thereto, have signed this Convention.

Done at Strasbourg, the 26 November 1987, in English and French, both texts being equally authentic, in a single copy which shall be deposited in the archives of the Council of Europe. The Secretary General of the Council of Europe shall transmit certified copies to each member State of the Council of Europe.

Annex – Privileges and immunities (Article 16)

1 For the purpose of this annex, references to members of the Committee shall be deemed to include references to experts mentioned in Article 7, paragraph 2.

2 The members of the Committee shall, while exercising their functions and during journeys made in the exercise of their functions, enjoy the following privileges and immunities:

    a immunity from personal arrest or detention and from seizure of their personal baggage and, in respect of words spoken or written and all acts done by them in their official capacity, immunity from legal process of every kind;

    b exemption from any restrictions on their freedom of movement on exit from and return to their country of residence, and entry into and exit from the country in which they exercise their functions, and from alien registration in the country which they are visiting or through which they are passing in the exercise of their functions.

3 In the course of journeys undertaken in the exercise of their functions, the members of the Committee shall, in the matter of customs and exchange control, be accorded:

    a by their own Government, the same facilities as those accorded to senior officials travelling abroad on temporary official duty;

    b by the Governments of other Parties, the same facilities as those accorded to representatives of foreign Governments on temporary official duty.

4 Documents and papers of the Committee, in so far as they relate to the business of the Committee, shall be inviolable.

The official correspondence and other official communications of the Committee may not be held up or subjected to censorship.

5 In order to secure for the members of the Committee complete freedom of speech and complete independence in the discharge of their duties, the immunity from legal process in respect of words spoken or written and all acts done by them in discharging their duties shall continue to be accorded, notwithstanding that the persons concerned are no longer engaged in the discharge of such duties.

6 Privileges and immunities are accorded to the members of the Committee, not for the personal benefit of the individuals themselves but in order to safeguard the independent exercise of their functions. The Committee alone shall be competent to waive the immunity of its members; it has not only the right, but is under a duty, to waive the immunity of one of its members in any case where, in its opinion, the immunity would impede the course of justice, and where it can be waived without prejudice to the purpose for which the immunity is accorded.

Protocol No. 1 to the European Convention for the Prevention of Torture and Inhuman or Degrading Treatment or Punishment
(European Treaty Series, No. 151)

Strasbourg, 4.XI.1993

The member States of the Council of Europe, signatories to this Protocol to the European Convention for the Prevention of Torture and Inhuman or Degrading Treatment or Punishment, signed at Strasbourg on 26 November 1987 (hereinafter referred to as "the Convention"),

Considering that non-member States of the Council of Europe should be allowed to accede to the Convention at the invitation of the Committee of Ministers,

Have agreed as follows:

Article 1

A sub-paragraph shall be added to Article 5, paragraph 1, of the Convention as follows:

"Where a member is to be elected to the Committee in respect of a non-member State of the Council of Europe, the Bureau of the Consultative Assembly shall invite the Parliament of that State to put forward three candidates, of whom two at least shall be its nationals. The election by the Committee of Ministers shall take place after consultation with the Party concerned."

Article 2

Article 12 of the Convention shall read as follows:

"Subject to the rules of confidentiality in Article 11, the Committee shall every year submit to the Committee of Ministers a general report on its activities which shall be transmitted to the Consultative Assembly and to any non-member State of the Council of Europe which is a party to the Convention, and made public."

Article 3

The text of Article 18 of the Convention shall become paragraph 1 of that article and shall be supplemented by the following second paragraph:

"2 The Committee of Ministers of the Council of Europe may invite any non-member State of the Council of Europe to accede to the Convention."

Article 4

In paragraph 2 of Article 19 of the Convention, the word "member" shall be deleted and the words "or approval," shall be replaced by "approval or accession.".

Article 5

In paragraph 1 of Article 20 of the Convention, the words "or approval" shall be replaced by "approval or accession,".

Article 6

1 The introductory sentence of Article 23 of the Convention shall read as follows:

"The Secretary General of the Council of Europe shall notify the member States and any non-member State of the Council of Europe party to the Convention of:"

2 In Article 23.b of the Convention, the words "or approval;" shall be replaced by "approval or accession;".

Article 7

1 This Protocol shall be open for signature by member States of the Council of Europe signatories to the Convention, which may express their consent to be bound by:

a signature without reservation as to ratification, acceptance or approval; or

b signature subject to ratification, acceptance or approval, followed by ratification, acceptance or approval.

2 Instruments of ratification, acceptance or approval shall be deposited with the Secretary General of the Council of Europe.

Article 8

This Protocol shall enter into force on the first day of the month following the expiration of a period of three months after the date on which all Parties to the Convention have expressed their consent to be bound by the Protocol, in accordance with the provisions of Article 7.

Article 9

The Secretary General of the Council of Europe shall notify the member States of the Council of Europe of:

a   any signature;

b   the deposit of any instrument of ratification, acceptance or approval;

c   the date of entry into force of this Protocol, in accordance with Article 8;

d   any other act, notification or communication relating to this Protocol.

In witness whereof, the undersigned, being duly authorised thereto, have signed this Protocol.

Done at Strasbourg this 4th day of November 1993, in English and French, both texts being equally authentic, in a single copy which shall be deposited in the archives of the Council of Europe. The Secretary General of the Council of Europe shall transmit certified copies to each member State of the Council of Europe.

Protocol No. 2 to the European Convention for the Prevention of Torture and Inhuman or Degrading Treatment or Punishment
(European Treaty Series, No.152)

Strasbourg, 4.XI.1993

The States, signatories to this Protocol to the European Convention for the Prevention of Torture and Inhuman or Degrading Treatment or Punishment, signed at Strasbourg on 26 November 1987 (hereinafter referred to as "the Convention"),

Convinced of the advisability of enabling members of the European Committee for the Prevention of Torture and Inhuman and Degrading Treatment or Punishment (hereinafter referred to as "the Committee") to be re-elected twice;

Also considering the need to guarantee an orderly renewal of the membership of the Committee,

Have agreed as follows:

Article 1

1   In Article 5, paragraph 3, the second sentence shall read as follows:

"They may be re-elected twice."

2   Article 5 of the Convention shall be supplemented by the following paragraphs 4 and 5:

"4 In order to ensure that, as far as possible, one half of the membership of the Committee shall be renewed every two years, the Committee of Ministers may decide, before proceeding to any subsequent election, that the term or terms of office of one or more members to be elected shall be for a period other than four years but not more than six and not less than two years.

5   In cases where more than one term of office is involved and the Committee of Ministers applies the preceding paragraph, the allocation of the terms of office shall be effected by the drawing of lots by the Secretary General, immediately after the election."

Article 2

This Protocol shall be open for signature by States signatories to the Convention or acceding thereto, which may express their consent to be bound by:

   a signature without reservation as to ratification, acceptance or approval; or

   b signature subject to ratification, acceptance or approval, followed by ratification, acceptance or approval.

2 Instruments of ratification, acceptance or approval shall be deposited with the Secretary General of the Council of Europe.

Article 3

This Protocol shall enter into force on the first day of the month following the expiration of a period of three months after the date on which all Parties to the Convention have expressed their consent to be bound by the Protocol, in accordance with the provisions of Article 2.

Article 4

The Secretary General of the Council of Europe shall notify the member States of the Council of Europe and non-member States Parties to the Convention of:

   a any signature;

   b the deposit of any instrument of ratification, acceptance or approval;

   c the date of any entry into force of this Protocol, in accordance with Article 3;

   d any other act, notification or communication relating to this Protocol.

In witness whereof, the undersigned, being duly authorised thereto, have signed this Protocol.

Done at Strasbourg, this 4th day of November 1993, in English and French, both texts being equally authentic, in a single copy which shall be deposited in the archives of the Council of Europe. The Secretary General of the Council of Europe shall transmit certified copies to each member State of the Council of Europe.

Explanatory report to the European Convention for the Prevention of Torture and Inhuman or Degrading Treatment or Punishment

I Introduction

1   On 28 September 1983 the Consultative Assembly of the Council of Europe adopted Recommendation 971 (1983) on the protection of detainees from torture and from cruel, inhuman or degrading treatment or punishment. In this text, the Assembly in particular recommended that the Committee of Ministers adopt the draft European Convention on the Protection of Detainees from Torture and from Cruel, Inhuman or Degrading Treatment or Punishment which was appended to the recommendation.

The background to this initiative may be summarised as follows:

2   In January 1981, the Assembly adopted Recommendation 909 (1981) on the International Convention against Torture, in which it referred to the work undertaken in the framework of the United Nations and recommended that the Committee of Ministers invite Governments of member States to hasten the adoption and implementation of the draft Convention against Torture being prepared by the United Nations Commission on Human Rights. It also invited the Governments of member States represented on that Commission to do their utmost to ensure that it gave detailed consideration to the draft optional Protocol to the Convention (submitted by Costa Rica), as soon as the draft Convention itself had been submitted to the United Nations Economic and Social Council.

3   In March 1981 two motions for resolutions on torture in member States of the Council of Europe were tabled in the Assembly, one by Mr Lidbom (Doc. 4718 rev.) and the other by Mr Jäger (Doc. 4730). These motions were transmitted to the Legal Affairs Commitee which decided to study them together.

4   Consideration by the Legal Affairs Committee resulted in a report (Doc. 5099) drawn up on behalf of the Committee by Mr Berrier and adopted on 30 June 1983. This report contained the draft of a European Convention elaborated by the International Commission of Jurists and the Swiss Committee against Torture at the request of the Rapporteur.

In September 1983, the opinion of the Political Affairs Committee on the report was presented by Mr Dejardin (Doc. 5123).

5 It is to be noted in this context that similar work was being conducted in the framework of the United Nations, and that the text of the Convention against Torture and other Cruel, Inhuman or Degrading Treatment or Punishment, referred to in Recommendation 909, was adopted by the General Assembly of the United Nations on 10 December 1984 and subsequently opened for signature. As to the draft optional Protocol submitted by Costa Rica, it aims to establish a preventive mechanism of a similar nature to that foreseen in the draft Convention appended to the Assembly's Recommendation 971.

6 Subsequent to the adoption of Recommendation 971, the Committee of Ministers conferred the following terms of reference on the Steering Committee for Human Rights (CDDH) at the 366th meeting of the Ministers' Deputies, in January 1984:

"Consider Assembly Recommendation 971 with a view to submitting to the Committee of Ministers, after consultation of the European Committee on Crime Problems (CDPC), the text of a draft Convention or other legal instrument on the protection of detainees from torture and from cruel, inhuman or degrading treatment or punishment."

7 The Committee of Experts for the extension of the rights embodied in the European Convention on Human Rights (DH-EX), a subordinate body of the CDDH, was instructed by the latter (15th meeting, March 1984) to implement this work under the authority of the CDDH.

8 The DH-EX considered the draft Convention appended to Recommendation 971 at its 19th to 25th meetings (May 1984 to June 1986). It took into account *inter alia* that:

– the Ministerial Conference on Human Rights (Vienna, 19-20 March 1985), in its Resolution No. 2, "urges the Committee of Ministers to have the work on a draft legal instrument on torture completed as rapidly as possible with a view to its adoption";

– the Final Communiqué of the 76th session of the Committee of Ministers (25 April 1985) said that the Ministers had "supported the Conference's appeal";

– in the Assembly, three questions concerning the draft Convention were put to the Chairman of the Committee of Ministers, one by Mr Berrier in January 1985, the others by Mr Arbeloa in April and September 1985;

– in the Final Communiqué of its 77th session (20 November 1985) the Committee of Ministers reiterated its great interest in the early completion of the draft Convention.

9 During its work, the DH-EX had occasion to consult the European Commission and Court of Human Rights. It also organised a hearing with representatives of the International Commission of Jurists, the Swiss Committee against Torture and the International Committee of the Red Cross. Other

hearings took place with two experts in the psychiatric field. Before transmitting in June 1986 the preliminary draft Convention to the CDDH, the DH-EX took into account the opinions of the European Committee for Legal Co-operation (CDCJ) and the European Committee on Crime Problems (CDPC) which had been consulted by the CDDH.

10 In addition to the CDCJ and the CDCP, the CDDH also consulted the European Commission and Court of Human Rights. The text of the draft European Convention for the prevention of torture and inhuman or degrading treatment or punishment was finalised at the CDDH's 21st meeting in November 1986 and then transmitted to the Committee of Ministers.

11 After having consulted the Assembly (see Opinion No. 133 of 27 March 1987), the Committee of Ministers adopted the text of the Convention on 26 June 1987. It was opened for signature by member States of the Council of Europe on 26 November 1987.

II Reasons for the elaboration of a new Convention

12 Torture and inhuman or degrading treatment or punishment are prohibited in national law and by several international instruments. Experience shows, however, that there is a need for wider and more effective international measures, in particular to strengthen the protection of persons deprived of their liberty.

13 Within the Council of Europe, the supervisory system established by the Convention for the Protection of Human Rights and Fundamental Freedoms, of 4 November 1950, has achieved important results. It is considered that this system, which is based on complaints from individuals or from States claiming that human rights violations have taken place, could usefully be supplemented by non-judicial machinery of a preventive character, whose task would be to examine the treatment of persons deprived of their liberty with a view to strengthening, if necessary, the protection of such persons from torture and from inhuman or degrading treatment or punishment.

14 For these reasons the present Convention establishes a Committee which may visit any place within the jurisdiction of the Parties where persons are deprived of their liberty by a public authority.

III Main features of the new system

15 As indicated in paragraphs 13 and 14 above, the Committee's function is to carry out visits and, where necessary, to suggest improvements as regards the protection of persons deprived of their liberty from torture and from inhuman or degrading treatment or punishment.

16 The members of the Committee will serve in their individual capacity and be chosen from among persons of high moral character, known for their competence in the field of human rights or having professional experience in the areas covered by the Convention. If the Committee considers it necessary, it may be assisted by suitably qualified experts.

17 It is not for the Committee to perform any judicial functions; it is not its task to adjudge that violations of the relevant international instruments have been committed. Accordingly, the Committee shall also refrain from expressing its views on the interpretation of those instruments either *in abstracto* or in relation to concrete facts.

18 When deciding whether there is a need for making recommendations, the Committee will, of course, have to assess the facts found during its visits. As the Committee is not competent to hear witnesses in conformity with general principles of judicial procedure, it will not have a sufficient basis for making recommendations if the facts are unclear and there is a need for further investigations. In such cases, the Committee may then inform the State concerned and suggest that further investigations be conducted at the national level and request to be kept informed of the results of the enquiry.

19 As a follow-up, the Committee may arrange for fresh visits to the places already visited.

20 In the application of the Convention, the Committee and the State concerned are obliged to co-operate. The purpose of the Committee is not to condemn States, but, in a spirit of co-operation and through advice, to seek improvements, if necessary, in the protection of persons deprived of their liberty.

IV Observations on the provisions of the Convention

Preamble

21 The preamble sets out reasons which led member States of the Council of Europe to adopt this Convention and states its purpose (see Chapters I to III above).

22 The reference to Article 3 of the European Convention on Human Rights will provide the Committee with a point of reference for its consideration of situations liable to give rise to torture or inhuman or degrading treatment or punishment (see *infra*, paragraphs 26 and 27).

Article 1

23 This article establishes the body which is to carry out the visits, and the purpose of the visits. In this way it describes the principal functions of the

European Committee for the Prevention of Torture and Inhuman or Degrading Treatment or Punishment.

24 The notion of "deprivation of liberty" for the purposes of the present Convention is to be understood within the meaning of Article 5 of the European Convention on Human Rights as elucidated by the case-law of the European Court and Commission of Human Rights. However, the distinction between "lawful" and "unlawful" deprivation of liberty arising in connection with Article 5 is immaterial in relation to the Committee's competence.

25 As already pointed out in paragraph 17, the Committee shall not perform any judicial functions: its members will not have to be lawyers, its recommendations will not bind the State concerned and the Committee shall not express any view on the interpretation of legal terms. Its task is a purely preventive one. It will carry out fact-finding visits, and, if necessary, on the basis of information obtained through them, make recommendations with a view to strengthening the protection of persons deprived of their libety from torture and from inhuman or degrading treatment or punishment.

26 The prohibition of torture and inhuman or degrading treatment or punishment is a general international standard which, albeit differently formulated, is found in various international instruments, such as Article 3 of the European Convention on Human Rights.

27 The case-law of the Court and Commission of Human Rights on Article 3 provides a source of guidance for the Committee. However, the Committee's activities are aimed at future prevention rather than the application of legal requirements to existing circumstances. The Committee should not seek to interfere in the interpretation and application of Article 3.

Article 2

28 By this provision Parties to the Convention agree to permit visits to any place within their jurisdiction where one or more persons are deprived of their liberty by a public authority. It is immaterial whether the deprivation is based on a formal decision or not.

29 Visits may take place in any circumstances. The Convention applies not only in peace time, but also during war or any other public emergency. The Committee's competence is, however, limited as regards the places it may visit by the provisions of Article 17, paragraph 3 (see *infra*, paragraph 93).

30 Visits may be organised in all kinds of places where persons are deprived of their liberty, whatever the reasons may be. The Convention is therefore applicable, for example, to places where persons are held in custody, are imprisoned as a result of conviction for an offence, are held in administrative detention, or are interned for medical reasons or where minors are detained by a public authority. Detention by military authorities is also covered by the Convention.

31 Visits to places where persons are deprived of their liberty because of their mental condition will require careful preparation and handling, for example as regards the qualifications and experience of those chosen for the visit and the manner in which the visit is conducted. In carrying out its visits, moreover, the Committee will no doubt wish to have regard to any relevant Recommendation adopted by the Committee of Ministers.

32 Visits may be carried out in private as well as public institutions. The criterion is whether the deprivation of liberty is the result of action by a public authority. Accordingly, the Committee may carry out visits only in relation to persons who are deprived of their liberty by a public authority, and not voluntary patients. However, in the latter case, it should be possible for the Committee to satisfy itself that this was indeed the wish of the patient concerned.

Article 3

33 As stated in the general considerations (see Chapters II and III above), the present Convention institutes a non-judicial system of a preventive character. It is not the task of the Committee to condemn States for violations, but to co-operate with them in strengthening the protection of persons deprived of their liberty. In order to indicate the spirit of the relationship between the Committee and the Parties, Article 3 contains a general provision on co-operation.

34 The principle of co-operation applies to all stages of the Committee's activities. It is of direct relevance to several other provisions of the Convention, such as Articles 2, 8, 9 and 10.

It is expected that the Committee will take advantage of national expertise made available to it by the Parties to assist its task, particularly during visits (see also *infra*, paragraphs 64 and 65).

Article 4

Paragraph 1

35 The Committee will be composed of a number of members amounting to the number of Parties to the Convention. This provision is inspired by the first part of Article 20 of the European Convention on Human Rights.

Paragraph 2

36 With regard to the qualifications of the members of the Committee it is stated in paragraph 2 that they shall be chosen from among persons of high moral character, known for their competence in the field of human rights or having professional experience in the areas covered by the Convention. It is not thought desirable to specify in detail the professional fields from which members of the Committee might be drawn. It is clear that they do not have

to be lawyers. It would be desirable that the Committee should include members who have experience in matters such as prison administration and the various medical fields relevant to the treatment of persons deprived of their liberty. This will make the dialogue between the Committee and the States more effective and facilitate concrete suggestions from the Committee.

Paragraph 3

37 This provision corresponds to the last part of Article 20 of the European Convention on Human Rights.

Paragraph 4

38 This paragraph requires that members serve in their individual capacity and that they are independent and impartial, and are to be available to serve the Committee effectively. Accordingly it is expected that candidates who would have a conflict of interests or who otherwise might encounter difficulties in satisfying the requirements of independence, impartiality and availability will not be proposed or elected. It is also expected that a member of the Committee who might have such difficulties with regard to an individual situation would not participate in any activity of the Committee relating to that situation.

Article 5

Paragraph 1

39 The procedure for the election of members of the Committee is basically the same as that laid down in Article 21 of the European Convention on Human Rights for the election of members of the Commission.

Paragraph 2

40 It is considered appropriate that the same electoral procedure should be followed for filling casual vacancies (death or resignation).

Paragraph 3

41 The term of office has been fixed at four years, with the possibility of re-election only once.

42 Provision is made for the partial renewal of the Committee after an initial period of two years. The procedure laid down is inspired by the corresponding provisions of Articles 22 and 40 of the European Convention on Human Rights.

Article 6

Paragraph 1

43 Having regard to the specific characteristics of the Committee's functions as provided for in the present Convention, it is specified that the Committee shall meet in camera. This provision complements the principle contained in Article 11 that the information gathered by the Committee in relation to a visit, its report and consultations with the State concerned shall be confidential.

44 Subject to the requirements laid down by Article 10, paragraph 2, the decisions of the Committee shall be taken by a majority of the members present. The quorum has been fixed at a number equal to a majority of the members.

Paragraph 2

45 This paragraph provides, in accordance with international practice, that the Committee shall draw up its own Rules of Procedure. They will regulate organisational matters normally found in such rules, including the election of the Chairman.

Paragraph 3

46 This provision, specifying that the Secretariat of the Committee shall be provided by the Secretary General of the Council of Europe, is inspired by the usual practice of this Organisation.

Article 7

Paragraph 1

47 This paragraph provides that it is the responsibility of the Committee to organise the visits to places referred to in Article 2 of the Convention. It also indicates that the Committee may organise periodic visits as well as *ad hoc* visits.

48 With regard to periodic visits, if it is to be effective the Committee will inevitably have to take into account the number of places to be visited in the States concerned. The Committee should also ensure, as far as possible, that the different States are visited on an equitable basis. Furthermore, its programme of periodic visits should not imply, for practical reasons, systematic visits in all places where persons are deprived of their liberty. The Committee should even accord a certain priority to *ad hoc* visits which appear to it to be required in the circumstances.

49 With regard to such *ad hoc* visits the Committee enjoys discretion as to when it deems a visit necessary and as to elements on which its decision is based. Thus, whilst the Committee should not be concerned with the

investigation of individual complaints (for which provision is already made, e.g. under the European Convention on Human Rights), it should be free to assess communications from individuals or groups of individuals and to decide whether to exercise its functions upon such communications. It should enjoy similar discretion in the event of a Party expressing the desire that the Committee should conduct a visit to places within its jurisdiction in order to investigate certain allegations and to clarify the situation.

Paragraph 2

50 The visits themselves need not necessarily be carried out by the full Committee; it is indeed probable that a visit by the full Committee would arise only in exceptional situations. Provision is therefore made in paragraph 2 for the visits to be carried out, as a general rule, by at least two members of the Committee, acting in the name of the latter. Exceptionally, however, the Committee may be represented by only one member, e.g. in *ad hoc* visits of an urgent nature when only one member is available.

51 If the Committee considers it necessary, it may be assisted by experts and interpreters. The underlying idea is to supplement the experience of the Committee by the assistance, for example, of persons who have special training or experience of humanitarian missions, who have a medical background or possess a special competence in the treatment of detainees or in prison regimes and, when appropriate, as regards young persons.

52 When organising a visit, the Committee will take into account the need to have at its disposal sufficient knowledge of the State concerned and its language.

53 The member or members of the Committee chosen to carry out a visit will enjoy the necessary authority for the contacts with the national authorities. They will have responsibility for the general conduct of the visit and for the findings submitted to the Committee after the visit.

Article 8

54 With the exception of paragraph 1, in which the reference to "Committee" means the plenary Committee, references to "Committee" in this Article (as in Articles 3, 9, 14, paragraph 3 and 17, paragraph 3) include the delegation carrying out the visit on behalf of the Committee.

Paragraph 1

55 By ratifying the Convention, the States are under an obligation to permit visits to any place within their jurisdiction. The purpose of the present provision is to specify the modalities by which a visit is initiated. Before a visit can take place the Committee shall notify the Government of the Party concerned of its intention to carry out a visit (cf. Article 15). After such

notification it may at any time visit any place referred to in Article 2 of the Convention.

It will be essential for the Committee and each Party to arrive at satisfactory arrangements as respects the credentials and means of identification of each person belonging to a visiting team.

56 This provision does not specify the period of time which should elapse (for example twenty-four or forty-eight hours) between the notification and the moment the visit becomes effective. Indeed, exceptional situations could arise in which the visit takes place immediately after the notification has been given. However, as a general rule and taking into consideration the principle of co-operation set out in Article 3, the Committee should give the State concerned reasonable time to take the necessary measures to make the visit as effective as possible. On the other hand, the Committee should carry out the visit within a reasonable time after the notification.

57 In the same spirit of co-operation, in cases where the notification announces the intention of the Committee to visit a State, without specifying the date and place of arrival, it is expected that the Committee will provide such details subsequently, before the visit takes place.

58 The notification should, in addition to announcing the visit, contain the names of members of the Committee and identify the experts taking part in the visit, the interpreters and other accompanying staff, as well as the places which the Committee intends visiting. However, the fact that specific establishments are mentioned in the notification should not preclude the Committee from announcing that it also wishes to visit other establishments in the course of the visit.

59 Finally, it is expected that the Committee will bear in mind that visits to high security prison establishments may require careful preparation.

Paragraph 2

60 It is understood, in view of the particular nature of the visits which the Committee is required to make, that this paragraph applies equally before, during and after visits. The paragraph contains an exhaustive list of the facilities with which the Committee is entitled to be provided by the Party. It is, however, understood that the Party should render the Committee other necessary assistance to facilitate its work.

61 Under sub-paragraph a, which must be read in conjunction with Articles 2 and 16, conditions prescribed by Parties with respect to immigration (e.g. visas) may not be invoked against members of the visiting team (subject to Article 14, paragraph 3 in respect of experts and other persons assisting the Committee). It is understood that the right to travel without restrictions does not give the Committee or its experts the general freedom to move within areas which are restricted for reasons of national defence (cf. Article 9).

62 Under sub-paragraph b, each Party must supply the Committee on request with a list of the places under its jurisdiction where persons deprived of their liberty are being held, stating the nature of the establishment (prison, police station, hospital, etc.). It is understood that, in supplying a list, the State concerned may provide a general description of places where persons are capable of being held from time to time, for example, all police stations or all military barracks, in addition to a specific list of permanent places where persons are deprived of their liberty, such as prisons and mental health institutions. It is envisaged that the Committee will eventually request a comprehensive list of places within a particular area which it intends to visit within the jurisdiction of the State. On the other hand, it is not necessary for the State to make a list of all detainees. If, for particular reasons, the Committee wishes to obtain information about a specific person (including his or her place of detention), it may ask for it under sub-paragraph d of this paragraph 2.

63 Sub-paragraph c emphasises the freedom of movement of the members of the Committee, particularly inside places referred to in Article 2. But this provision does not prevent the Committee from being accompanied by an official from the visited State, in order to assist with the visit (cf. Article 15). The State may in particular require the Committee to be accompanied by a senior officer in places which are secret for reasons of national defence or which enjoy special protection for reasons of national security (cf. Article 9). However, an accompanying person must not be present at the interviews in private mentioned in paragraph 3 of this Article.

64 Sub-paragraph d obliges Parties to provide the Committee with information available to them which is necessary for the Committee to carry out its task. Access to information will clearly be of great importance to the Committee. At the same time, it is acknowledged that particular rules concerning disclosure of information may be applicable in member States. Accordingly, the Committee is for its part obliged, when seeking information from a Party, to have regard to applicable rules of national law and professional ethics (in particular rules regarding data protection and rules of medical secrecy). It is envisaged that possible difficulties in this field will be resolved in the spirit of mutual understanding and co-operation upon which the Convention is founded.

65 It is understood that it is for Parties to decide the form (e.g. originals or copies of documents) in which the information requested by the Committee shall be communicated.

Paragraph 3

66 Under this paragraph the Committee may conduct interviews in private. For the purpose of such interviews it can choose its own interpreters and must not be subjected to any time-limits.

The Committee should take special care in connection with mentally disturbed patients over the number, qualifications and linguistic ability of the person or persons conducting the interview (cf. paragraph 31 *supra*).

67 It is understood that a person deprived of liberty is not obliged to agree to enter into contact with the Committee. But the latter must be given the opportunity to satisfy itself that this is in fact the free decision of the person concerned.

Paragraph 4

68 When referring to persons with whom the Committee may communicate, those drafting the Convention had in mind in particular the families, lawyers, doctors and nursing staff of the persons deprived of their liberty. But no private individuals can be obliged to communicate with the Committee.

69 However, this right conferred on the Committee does not authorise it to organise formal hearings in the legal sense with all the procedural conditions that this would imply. For instance, no one would be obliged to give evidence on oath.

Paragraph 5

70 This paragraph enables the Committee to make certain observations during the visit itself. This possibility should only be made use of in exceptional cases (e.g. when there is an urgent need to improve the treatment of persons deprived of liberty). It will not absolve the Committee from making a subsequent report as provided for in Article 10.

Article 9

71 This article recognises that, notwithstanding the obligations of a Party to permit visits by the Committee, certain exceptional circumstances may justify a postponement of a visit or some limitation of the right of access of the Committee as regards a particular place. Paragraph 1 specifies these exceptional circumstances, restricting the grounds on which the Article may be invoked on any particular occasion to:

- safeguarding national defence;
- safeguarding public safety which, it is envisaged, would include an urgent and compelling need to prevent serious crime;
- serious disorder in prisons and other places where persons are deprived of their liberty;
- cases where, having regard to the medical (including mental) condition of a person proposed to be visited, a visit at a particular time could prove detrimental to health;
- avoiding prejudicing an urgent interrogation, and consequential investigation, relating to a serious crime.

72 A Party which wishes to invoke the provisions of Article 9 is required to make representations as to the relevant circumstances to the Committee. The Committee and the Party would then be required by paragraph 2 to enter into consultations to elucidate the circumstances cited by the Party and their bearing on the proposals notified by the Committee pursuant to Article 8. The Committee and the Party are also required (and this is a particular example of the co-operation enjoined by Article 3) to seek agreement on ways in which the Committee will be able to perform its functions speedily and effectively. One possibility which is specified in the Article is that if, for example, representations are made on national security grounds against a visit to a particular place, any person who is deprived of his liberty in that place shall be transferred to another place where he may be visited by the Committee. This paragraph also provides that when a visit to any place is postponed, the Party shall ensure that the Committee is fully informed about the persons who are deprived of their liberty at that place.

Article 10

Paragraph 1

73 This paragraph deals with the report which the Committee has to draw up following each visit. This will be based on the facts found during the visit and will take account of any observations which the State concerned might wish to make. The report will also contain the recommendations the Committee considers necessary, the object being in every case to strengthen the protection of persons deprived of their liberty. It is understood that the report transmitted to the State concerned will not necessarily contain all the information obtained by the Committee on the occasion of its visits (e.g. records of certain interviews).

Paragraph 2

74 In certain eventualities referred to in this paragraph the Committee may, after the State concerned has had an opportunity to make known its views, decide to make a public statement. The exceptional competence of the Committee to make a public statement can be used if the State fails to co-operate or refuses to improve the situation in the light of the Committee's recommendations. Given the importance of such a decision, it may only be taken by a qualified majority. Before using this remedy in the case of a State's refusal to improve the situation, the Committee should pay full regard to any difficulties in the way of doing so.

75 The Committee will have a wide discretion in deciding what information to make public, but will have to take due account of the need to secure that information passed over in confidence is not revealed. It should also take into consideration the desirability of not revealing information in connection with pending investigations.

Article 11

Paragraph 1

76 This provision establishes the principle of the confidential nature of the Committee's activities. The "information gathered by the Committee" may consist of facts it has itself observed, information which it has obtained from external sources and information which it has itself collected.

Paragraph 2

77 This provision specifies that, whenever requested to do so by the State concerned, the Committee is required to publish the report and any comments the State wishes to make. If the State concerned itself makes the report public, it should do so in its entirety.

Paragraph 3

78 This paragraph provides that no personal data may be published without the express consent of the person concerned. But this might not exclude the publication of such data if the identity of the person concerned is not revealed or could not be discovered from the context.

Article 12

79 Every year the Committee shall submit a general report on its activities to the Committee of Ministers. The report, which will be transmitted to the Assembly and made public, should contain information on the organisation and internal workings of the Committee and on its activities proper, with particular mention of the States visited. When preparing its report, the Committee must naturally comply with the provisions of Article 11 concerning the confidential character of certain types of information and data.

Article 13

80 In accordance with this provision, members of the Committee, experts and other persons assisting the Committee are required to observe confidentiality, even after their term of office has come to an end. It relates to all facts or information which may have come to the notice of the Committee members or such other persons during the discharge of their functions when visits are being effected, or at any other moment.

Article 14

Paragraph 1

81 This provision lays down the principle that the names of persons assisting the Committee shall be specified in the notification of a visit under Article 8, paragraph 1.

Paragraph 2

82 The experts shall be bound by the same duties of independence, impartiality and availability as the members of the Committee (cf. Article 4, paragraph 4). They are subject to the instructions of the Committee and shall act under its authority.

Paragraph 3

83 This paragraph sets forth the conditions in which a State may refuse to a person assisting the Committee the possibility of participating in visits, or in a particular visit, to a place within its jurisdiction.

84 This right may be exercised only exceptionally and at the earliest opportunity. Thus a State, upon being given the relevant information, should only refuse such a person if, in its opinion, he fails to fulfil the requirements set forth in paragraph 2 of this Article or in Article 13. This might be the case if the person concerned has manifested a biased attitude towards that State or if, on other occasions, he has broken the rule of confidentiality.

85 When a State declares that a person may not take part in a visit, the Committee may wish to ask for the reasons, on the understanding that the enquiry and any response shall be confidential. Such an arrangement may be of assistance to the Committee in appointing other persons to assist it.

86 If, in the course of the visit, a person assisting the Committee behaves in a manner that the State concerned considers improper (for instance, if he makes political or similar public statements), it may request the Committee to take all the measures the latter deems appropriate.

Article 15

87 In order to facilitate the notifications under Article 8, paragraph 1 of the Convention, the present provision obliges Parties to inform the Committee of the authority to which such notifications should be sent. A Party must also inform the Committee of the name of any liaison officer it may appoint to facilitate the task of the Committee when making a visit.

Article 16

88 This article deals with the privileges and immunities of the Committee, its members and experts. It is inspired by Article 59 of the European Convention on Human Rights and by the Second and Fourth Protocols to the General Agreement on Privileges and Immunities of the Council of Europe.

Article 17

Paragraph 1

89 This paragraph provides that the present Convention cannot be invoked as a justification for restricting the protection granted under other international instruments or at the domestic level. Indeed, the Convention is only one of several measures aimed at preventing torture and strengthening the protection afforded to persons deprived of their liberty.

90 The fact that national authorities may be empowered to conduct certain investigations in the places covered by the Convention is not sufficient to prevent the Committee from deciding to conduct a visit. But in the spirit of co-operation which is to govern the application of the Convention, the Committee may wish to enter into contact with such national authorities before making a decision (cf. paragraphs 33 and 34 above).

Paragraph 2

91 This paragraph addresses the particular relationship between the new Convention and the European Convention on Human Rights, to which all member States of the Council of Europe are party and a connection with which is acknowledged in the preamble. The obligations of the Parties under the European Convention on Human Rights are not affected. Nor is the competence entrusted by that Convention to the Court and Commission of Human Rights and the Committee of Ministers. Accordingly, in respecting the established competence of these organs, the Committee set up by the present Convention will not concern itself with matters raised in proceedings pending before them, and will not itself formulate interpretations of the provisions of the European Convention on Human Rights.

92 In particular, the cardinal importance of the right of individual petition under Article 25 of the European Convention on Human Rights remains undiminished. Accordingly, it is not envisaged that a person whose case has been examined by the Committee would be met with a plea based on Article 27, paragraph 1 (b) of the European Convention on Human Rights if he subsequently lodges a petition with the Commission of Human Rights alleging that he has been the victim of a violation of that Convention.

Paragraph 3

93 It follows from Article 2 that the Convention applies both in time of peace and in time of war. However, it appeared necessary to take account of the existence of other international instruments, in particular the Geneva Conventions of 12 August 1949 and the 8 June 1977 Protocols. In the case of armed conflict (international or non-international) the Geneva Conventions must have priority of application; that is to say that the visits will be carried out by the delegates or representatives of the International Committee

of the Red Cross (ICRC) (However, the new Committee could proceed to visit certain places where (particularly in the event of non-international armed conflict) the ICRC does not visit them "effectively" or "on a regular basis". On the other hand, visits to detainees made by the ICRC in time of peace in a specific country by virtue of bilateral agreements (outside the framework of the Geneva Convention) are not covered by this provision. In such cases the Committee must decide what attitude to adopt taking account of the situation and status of persons who might be the subject of a visit.

94 The drafters of the Convention decided to make a distinction with regard to the Geneva Conventions, not only because of the specific competence and experience acquired by the ICRC but also because the latter carries out functions and uses methods very similar to those of the new Committee. Thus it seemed particularly necessary to specify the respective competence of the two organs.

Articles 18 to 23

95 These articles, which contain the final clauses of the Convention, correspond to the model adopted by the Committee of Ministers of the Council of Europe.

As for Article 21, it should be noted that the option excluding the possibility of making reservations has been chosen.

Rules of Procedure of the European Committee for the Prevention of Torture and Inhuman or Degrading Treatment or Punishment

(Adopted on 16 November 1989 and amended on 8 March 1990, 11 May 1990, 9 November 1990, 31 January 1991, 20 September 1991, and 12 March 1997)

The Committee,

Having regard to the European Convention for the Prevention of Torture and Inhuman or Degrading Treatment or Punishment (hereinafter referred to as "the Convention");

Pursuant to Article 6, paragraph 2, of the Convention,

Adopts the present Rules :

Title I – Organisation of the Committee

Chapter I – Members of the Committee

Rule 1

(Calculation of term of office)

1   The duration of the term of office of a member of the Committee shall be calculated as from his election, unless the Committee of Ministers stipulates otherwise when proceeding to the election.[1]

2   A member elected to replace a member whose term of office has not expired shall be elected for a four year term of office.

Rule 2

(Solemn declaration)

Before taking up his duties, each member of the Committee shall, at the first meeting of the Committee at which he is present after his election, make the following solemn declaration:

---

1. Paragraph amended by the Committee on 12 March 1997.

"I solemnly declare that I will exercise my functions as a member of this Committee honourably, independently, impartially and conscientiously and that I will keep secret all Committee proceedings".

Rule 3

(Precedence)

1 Members of the Committee shall take precedence after the President and Vice-Presidents according to the length of time they have been in office.

2 Members having the same length of time in office shall take precedence according to age.

3 Re-elected members shall take precedence having regard to the duration of their previous term of office.

Rule 4

(Resignation)

Resignation of a member of the Committee shall be notified to the President, who shall transmit it to the Secretary General of the Council of Europe.

Chapter II – Presidency of the Committee

Rule 5

(Election of the President and Vice-Presidents)

1 The Committee shall elect from among its members a President and a first and second Vice-President.

2 The President and Vice-Presidents shall be elected for a term of two years. They may be re-elected. However, the term of office of the President or of a Vice-President shall end if he ceases to be a member of the Committee.

3 If the President or a Vice-President ceases to be a member of the Committee or resigns his office of President or Vice-President before its normal expiry, the Committee may elect a successor for the remainder of the term of that office.

4 The elections referred to in this Rule shall be held by secret ballot. Election shall be by a majority of the members present.

5 If no candidate is elected after the first ballot, a second ballot shall take place between the two candidates who have received most votes ; in the case of equal voting, the candidate having precedence under Rule 3 shall take part in the second ballot. If necessary, a third ballot shall take place between the two candidates concerned. The candidate who receives the

most votes in such a third ballot or, in the case of equal voting, who has precedence under Rule 3, shall be declared elected.

6   If there are only two candidates for a vacant office and neither of the candidates is elected after the first ballot, a second ballot shall take place. The candidate who receives the most votes in such a second ballot or, in the case of equal voting, who has precedence under Rule 3, shall be declared elected.

Rule 6

(Functions of the President)

1   The President shall chair the meetings of the Committee and shall perform all other functions conferred upon him by these Rules of Procedure and by the Committee.

2   In exercising his functions, the President shall remain under the authority of the Committee.

3   The President may delegate certain of his functions to either Vice-President.

Rule 7

(Functions of the Vice-Presidents)

The first Vice-President shall take the place of the President if the latter is unable to carry out his duties or if the office of President is vacant. The second Vice-President shall replace the first Vice-President if the latter is unable to carry out his duties or if the office of first Vice-President is vacant.

Rule 8

(Replacement of the President and Vice-Presidents)

If the President and Vice-Presidents are at the same time unable to carry out their duties or if their offices are at the same time vacant, the duties of President shall be carried out by another member of the Committee according to the order of precedence laid down in Rule 3.

Rule 9

(Obstacle to the exercise of the functions of President)

No member of the Committee shall preside when the report on a visit to the State Party in respect of which he was elected is being considered.

Chapter III – Bureau of the Committee

Rule 10

1   The Bureau of the Committee shall consist of the President and Vice-Presidents. If one or more members of the Bureau are unable to carry out their duties, they shall be replaced by other members of the Committee in accordance with the rules of precedence laid down in Rule 3.

2   The Bureau shall direct the work of the Committee and shall perform all other functions conferred upon it by these Rules of Procedure and by the Committee.

Chapter IV – Secretariat of the Committee

Rule 11

The Secretariat of the Committee shall consist of a Secretary and other staff members appointed by the Secretary General of the Council of Europe.

Title II – Working of the Committee : general rules

Chapter I – Seat of the Committee and languages

Rule 12

(Seat of the Committee)

The seat of the Committee shall be in Strasbourg.

Rule 13

(Languages)

The official and working languages of the Committee shall be English and French.

Chapter II – Meetings of the Committee

Rule 14

(Holding of meetings)

1   The Committee and its Bureau shall hold such meetings as are required for the exercise of their functions.

2   Committee meetings shall be convened at dates decided by the Committee. The Committee shall meet at other times by decision of the Bureau, as circumstances may require. It shall also meet if at least one third of the members so request.

3   The Secretary shall notify the members of the Committee of the date, time and place of each Committee meeting. Whenever possible, such notification shall be given at least six weeks in advance.

Rule 15

(Agenda)

1   Following consultation with the Bureau, the Secretary shall transmit to the members a draft agenda simultaneously with the notification of the meeting.

2   The agenda shall be adopted by the Committee at the beginning of the meeting.

Rule 16

(Meeting documentation)

The Secretary shall transmit to the members of the Committee the working documents relating to the different agenda items, whenever possible at least four weeks in advance.

Rule 17

(Quorum)

The quorum of the Committee shall be the majority of its members.

Rule 18

(Privacy of meetings)

1   The Committee shall meet in camera. Its deliberations shall remain confidential.

2   Apart from members of the Committee, only members of the Committee's Secretariat, interpreters and persons providing technical assistance to the Committee may be present at its meetings, unless the Committee decides otherwise.

Rule 19

(Hearings)

The Committee may hear any person whom it considers to be in a position to assist it in the performance of its functions under the Convention.

Chapter III – Conduct of business

Rule 20

(Proposals)

A proposal must be submitted in writing if a member of the Committee so requests. In that case it shall not be discussed until it has been circulated.

Rule 21

(Order of voting on proposals and amendments)

1   Where a number of proposals relate to the same subject, they shall be put to the vote in the order in which they were submitted. In case of doubt, the President shall decide.

2   Where a proposal is the subject of an amendment, the amendment shall be put to the vote first. Where two or more amendments to the same proposal are presented, the Committee shall vote first on whichever departs furthest in substance from the original proposal, and so on until all the amendments have been put to the vote. However, where the acceptance of one amendment necessarily entails rejection of another, the latter shall not be put to the vote. The final vote shall then be taken on the proposal as amended or not amended. In case of doubt as to the order of priority, the President shall decide.

3   Parts of a proposal or amendment may be put to the vote separately.

4   In the case of proposal with financial implications, the most costly shall be put to the vote first.

Rule 22

(Order of procedural motions)

Procedural motions shall take precedence over all other proposals or motions except points of order. They shall be put to the vote in the following order:

    a   suspension of the meeting;

    b   adjournment of the meeting;

    c   adjournment of discussion on the item in hand;

    d   closure of discussion on the item in hand.

Rule 23

(Reconsideration of a question)

When a decision has been taken it is only re-examined if a member of the Committee so requests and the Committee accedes to this request.

Rule 24

(Voting)

1   Subject to the provisions of Rules 44 (paragraph 1), 47, 48, 50 and 51, the decisions of the Committee shall be taken by a majority of the members present.

2   In matters other than elections, a proposal shall be regarded as rejected if the majority referred to in paragraph 1 is not obtained.

3   Subject to Rule 5, paragraph 4, the Committee shall normally vote by show of hands. However, any member may request that a vote be taken by roll-call; in this event, the roll shall be called in the alphabetical order of the names of the Committee's members, beginning with the letter 'A'.

4   After a vote has commenced, there shall be no interruption of the voting except on a point of order by a member in connection with the actual conduct of the voting. Brief statements by members consisting solely of explanations of their votes may be permitted by the President before the voting has commenced or after the voting has been completed.

Chapter IV – Decisions and meeting reports

Rule 25

(Decisions)

At the end of each meeting the Secretary shall submit to the Committee for its approval a list of the decisions adopted during the meeting.

Rule 26

(Meeting reports)

1   A draft report of the Committee's deliberations at each meeting shall be prepared by the Secretary. The draft report shall be circulated as soon as possible to members of the Committee, who will be given the opportunity to submit corrections within a prescribed time-limit.

2   If no corrections are submitted, the meeting report shall be deemed to be adopted. If corrections are submitted, they shall be consolidated in a single document and circulated to all members. In this latter case, the adoption of the meeting report shall be taken up at the next meeting of the Committee.

Chapter V – Working parties

Rule 27

The Committee may setup *ad hoc* working parties comprising a limited number of its members. The terms of reference of such working parties shall be defined by the Committee.

Chapter VI – Communications containing information submitted for the Committee's consideration

Rule 28

1 The Secretary shall bring to the Committee's attention communications received containing information submitted for the Committee's consideration, unless the information in question relates to matters which manifestly fall outside its field of competence.

2 Such communications received by individual members of the Committee shall be forwarded to the Secretariat.

3 The Secretary shall keep a register of all communications received.

4 The Secretary shall send an acknowledgement of receipt to the authors of such communications.

Title III – Procedure concerning visits

Chapter I – Basic rules

Rule 29

(The principle of visits)

Pursuant to Article 1 and 7 of the Convention, the Committee shall organise visits to places referred to in Article 2 of the Convention to examine the treatment of persons deprived of their liberty, with a view to strengthening, if necessary, the protection of such persons from torture and from inhuman or degrading treatment or punishment.

Rule 30[1]

(Requests for information or explanations)

1 Before deciding on a particular visit, the Committee or, if appropriate, the Bureau may request information or explanations as regards the general situation in the State concerned, as regards a given place, or as regards an isolated case concerning which it has received reports.

---

1. Rule inserted by the Committee on 8 March 1990.

2 Following receipt of such information or explanations, details of remedial action taken by the national authorities may be requested.

Rule 31

(Periodic visits)

1 The Committee shall carry out visits of a periodic nature.

2 Before the end of each calendar year, the Committee shall establish a provisional programme of periodic visits for the following calendar year. In drawing up this programme the Committee shall ensure, as far as possible, that the different States Parties to the Convention are visited on an equitable basis, regard being had to the number of relevant places in each State Party[1].

3 The Committee may subsequently decide to modify the above-mentioned programme in the light of circumstances.

4 The Commmittee shall make public the names of the countries in which periodic visits are envisaged in a given year, after having informed the authorities of each of the States concerned of the likelihood of a visit[2].

Rule 32

(Ad hoc visits)

1 In addition to periodic visits, the Committee may carry out such *ad hoc* visits as appear to it to be required in the circumstances.

2 When the Committee is not in session, the Bureau may, in case of urgency, decide on the Committee's behalf on the carrying out of an ad hoc visit. The President shall report to the Committee at its next meeting on any action which has been taken under this paragraph.

Rule 33

(Follow-up visits)

The Committee may carry out one or more follow-up visits to any place already visited in the context of a periodic or *ad hoc* visit.

Rule 34

(Responsibility for carrying out visits)

1 As a general rule, visits shall be carried out by a delegation of the Committee consisting of at least two of its members. Exceptionally, visits may be carried out by the full Committee or by a single member thereof.

---

1. Paragraph amended by the Committee on 31 January 1991.
2. Paragraph inserted by the Committee on 11 May 1990 and amended on 31 January 1991.

2 The members of the Committee with responsibility for carrying out a visit shall act in the name of the Committee.

Rule 35

(Notification of visits)

1 The Committee or, if the Committee is not in session at the relevant time, its President shall notify the Government of the Party concerned of the intention to carry out a visit. The notification shall be sent to the authority referred to in Article 15 of the Convention.

2 The notification shall contain the names of the Committee members responsible for carrying out the visit and of all persons assisting the visiting delegation.

3 The notification shall indicate the places which the delegation intends to visit. However, this shall not prevent the visiting delegation from deciding to visit also places not indicated in the notification.

4 The notification of a visit in pursuance of paragraphs 1 to 3 may be given in stages.[1]

Rule 36

(Register of visits)

The Secretary shall maintain a register of all visits carried out by the Committee.

Chapter II – Visiting delegations

Rule 37

(Choice of members)

1 The members of the Committee to carry out a visit shall be chosen by the Committee or, in case of urgency when the Committee is not in session, by the Bureau. Due regard shall be had to the nature of the visit in question, and in particular to the type of place or places to be visited, when the composition of the delegation is determined.

2 The member of the Committee elected in respect of the State to be visited shall not be chosen as a member of the visiting delegation[2].

3 In consultation with the Bureau, the members of the delegation shall appoint one of their number as Head of the delegation[3].

---

1. Paragraph inserted by the Committee on 8 March 1990.
2. Paragraph inserted by the Committee on 9 November 1990.
3. Paragraph amended by the Committee on 31 January 1991.

Rule 38

(Assistants)

1   The Committee or, in the case of an ad hoc visit under Rule 32, paragraph 2, the Bureau may decide that a visiting delegation shall be assisted by one or more experts or interpreters.

2   As a rule, a visiting delegation shall not be assisted by an expert who is a national of the State to be visited[1].

3   At least one member of the Secretariat of the Committee shall accompany each visiting delegation.

4   All persons assisting a visiting delegation shall act on the instructions and under the authoritiy of the Head of the delegation.

Rule 39

(Procedure for visits)

1   Visiting delegations shall carry out visits in accordance with any general or specific instructions or guidelines issued by the Committee or, as the case may be, the Bureau.

2   A visiting delegation may immediately communicate observations to the authorities of the Party concerned.

Rule 40

(Visiting delegation reports)

On the completion of its visit, a visiting delegation shall as soon as possible submit a report to the Committee. This report shall contain in particular:

–   a description of the different stages of the visit;

–   an account of the facts found during the visit and of consultations with the authorities of the Party concerned, that are of relevance for the Committee's report;[2]

–   proposals for any recommendations which the visiting delegation considers should be addressed to the Party.

---

1. Paragraph inserted by the Committee on 9 November 1990.
2. Indent amended by the Committee on 31 January 1991.

Title IV – Post-visit procedure

Chapter I – Reports and recommendations

Rule 41

(Preparation of the Committee's report)

1   After each visit the Committee shall draw up, in the light of the visiting delegation's report, a report for transmission to the Party concerned. This report shall set out the facts found during the visit and contain any recommendations which the Committee considers necessary with a view to strengthening the protection of persons deprived of their liberty.

2   When drawing up its report, the Committee shall take account of any observations which the Party concerned might submit to it following a visit. Further, the Committee may on its own initiative seek observations or additional information from the Party.

3   After its adoption, the report shall be transmitted to the Party concerned by the President.

Rule 42

(Confidential nature of the report)

1   The report transmitted to a Party following a visit is and, as a rule, shall remain confidential. However, the Committee shall publish its report, together with any comments of the Party concerned, whenever requested to do so by that Party.

2   If the Party itself makes the report public, but does not do so in its entirety, the Committee may decide to publish the whole report.

3   Similarly, the Committee may decide to publish the whole report if the Party concerned makes a public statement summarising the report or commenting upon its contents.[1]

4   Publication of the report by the Committee under paragraphs 1 to 3 of this Rule shall be subject to the provisions of Rule 45, paragraph 2.[2]

Rule 43

(Subsequent consultations)

After transmission of the Committee's report, the Committee and the Party may hold consultations concerning in particular the implementation of any recommendations set out in the report.

---

1. Paragraph inserted by the Committee on 20 September 1991.
2. Paragraph amended by the Committee on 20 September 1991.

Chapter II – Public statements

Rule 44

1 If a Party fails to co-operate with the Committee or refuses to improve the situation in the light of the Committee's recommendations, the Committee may decide, by a majority of two-thirds of its members, to make a public statement on the matter.

2 Before a decision to make such a statement is taken, the Party concerned shall be given an opportunity to make known its views.

3 Subject to the provisions of Rule 45, paragraph 2, the Committee shall be released from the obligation of confidentiality set out under Title V when making a public statement.

Title V – Confidentiality

Rule 45

1 Subject to Rules 42 and 44, information gathered by the Committee in relation to a visit, its report on that visit, and its consultations with the Party concerned shall be and shall remain confidential. The same shall apply to all Committee meeting reports and working documents.

2 No personal data shall be published without the express consent of the person concerned.

Rule 46

1 Members of the Committee, experts and other persons assisting the Committee are required, during and after their terms of office, to maintain the confidentiality of the facts or information of which they have become aware during the discharge of their functions.

2 A provision to the above effect shall be inserted in the contracts of experts and interpreters recruited to assist the Committee.

Rule 47[1]

If there are serious grounds for believing that a Committee member has violated the obligation of confidentiality, the Committee may, after the member concerned has had an opportunity to state his views, decide by a majority of two-thirds of its members to inform the Committee of Ministers of the matter.

---

1. Rule inserted by the Committee on 9 November 1990.

Rule 48[1]

1 If there are serious grounds for believing that a member of the Committee's Secretariat or an interpreter has violated the obligation of confidentiality, the Committee may, after the person concerned has had an opportunity to state his views, decide by a majority of its members to inform the Secretary General of the Council of Europe of the matter and request that appropriate measures be taken.

2 If there are serious grounds for believing that an expert has violated the obligation of confidentiality, the Committee shall, after the person concerned has had an opportunity to state his views, decide by a majority of its members on the measures to be taken.

Title VI – Annual general report of the committee

Rule 49

1 Subject to the obligation of confidentiality set out under Title V, the Committee shall every year submit to the Committee of Ministers a general report on its activities, which shall be transmitted to the Consultative Assembly and made public.

2 The report shall contain *inter alia* information on the organisation and internal workings of the Committee and on its activities proper, with particular mention of the States visited.

3 Whenever possible, the report shall be adopted at the first meeting of the Committee in a given calendar year and cover the whole of the preceding calendar year. The Secretary shall submit a draft report to the Committee in good time.

Title VII – Amendments and suspension

Rule 50

(Amendment of the Rules)

These Rules of Procedure may be amended by decision taken by a majority of the members of the Committee, subject to the provisions of the Convention.

---

1. Rule inserted by the Committee on 9 November 1990.

Rule 51

(Suspension of a Rule)

Upon the proposal of a Committee member, the application of a Rule may be suspended by decisions taken by a majority of the members of the Committee, subject to the provisions of the Convention. The suspension of a rule shall be limited in its operation to the particular purpose for which such suspension has been sought.

European Convention for the Prevention of Torture and Inhuman or Degrading Treatment or Punishment and protocols: signatures and ratifications at 1 January 1999

Member state	CPT		Protocol No. 1		Protocol No. 2	
	Signed	Ratified	Signed	Ratified	Signed	Ratified
Albania	02/10/96	02/10/96	02/10/96	02/10/96	02/10/96	02/10/96
Andorra	10/09/96	06/01/97	—	**	—	**
Austria	26/11/87	06/01/89	04/11/93	30/04/96	04/11/93	30/04/96
Belgium	26/11/87	23/07/91	04/11/93	12/09/96	04/11/93	12/09/96
Bulgaria	30/09/93	03/05/94	04/03/97	27/10/97	04/03/97	27/10/97
Croatia	06/11/96	11/10/97	—	**	—	**
Cyprus	26/11/87	03/04/89	02/02/94	10/09/97	02/02/94	10/09/97
Czech Republic*	23/12/92	07/09/95	28/04/95	07/09/95	28/04/95	07/09/95
Denmark	26/11/87	02/05/89	04/11/93	26/04/94	04/11/93	26/04/94
Estonia	28/06/96	06/11/96	28/06/96	06/11/96	28/06/96	06/11/96
Finland	16/11/89	20/12/90	04/11/93	04/11/93	04/11/93	04/11/93
France	26/11/87	09/01/89	04/11/93	19/08/98	04/11/93	14/08/96
Germany	26/11/87	21/02/90	04/11/93	13/12/96	04/11/93	13/12/96
Greece	26/11/87	02/08/91	04/11/93	29/06/94	04/11/93	29/06/94
Hungary	09/02/93	04/11/93	04/11/93	04/11/93	04/11/93	04/11/93
Iceland	26/11/87	19/06/90	08/09/94	29/06/95	08/09/94	29/06/95
Ireland	14/03/88	14/03/88	10/04/96	10/04/96	10/04/96	10/04/96
Italy	26/11/87	29/12/88	30/10/96	**	30/10/96	**
Latvia	11/09/97	10/02/98	11/09/97	10/02/98	11/09/97	10/02/98
Liechtenstein	26/11/87	12/09/91	04/11/93	05/05/95	04/11/93	05/05/95
Lithuania	14/09/95	26/11/98	14/09/95	26/11/98	14/09/95	26/11/98

Luxembourg	26/11/87	06/09/88	04/11/93	20/07/95	04/11/93	20/07/95
Malta	26/11/87	07/03/88	04/11/93	04/11/93	04/11/93	04/11/93
Moldova	02/05/96	02/10/97	02/10/97	02/10/97	02/10/97	02/10/97
Netherlands	26/11/87	12/10/88	05/05/94	23/02/95	05/05/94	23/02/95
Norway	26/11/87	21/04/89	04/11/93	04/11/93	04/11/93	04/11/93
Poland	11/07/94	10/10/94	11/01/95	24/03/95	11/01/95	24/03/95
Portugal	26/11/87	29/03/90	03/06/94	20/03/98	03/06/94	**
Romania	04/11/93	04/10/94	04/11/93	04/10/94	04/11/93	04/10/94
Russian Federation	28/02/96	05/05/98	28/02/96	05/05/98	28/02/96	05/05/98
San Marino	16/11/89	31/01/90	04/11/93	05/12/96	04/11/93	05/12/96
Slovakia*	23/12/92	11/05/94	07/03/94	11/05/94	07/03/94	11/05/94
Slovenia	04/11/93	02/02/94	31/03/94	16/02/95	31/03/94	16/02/95
Spain	26/11/87	02/05/89	21/02/95	08/06/95	21/02/95	08/06/95
Sweden	26/11/87	21/06/88	07/03/94	07/03/94	07/03/94	07/03/94
Switzerland	26/11/87	07/10/88	09/03/94	09/03/94	09/03/94	09/03/94
"The former Yugoslav Republic of Macedonia"	14/06/96	06/06/97	14/06/96	06/06/97	14/06/96	06/06/97
Turkey	11/01/88	26/02/88	10/05/95	17/09/97	10/05/95	17/09/97
Ukraine	02/05/96	05/05/97	26/01/98	**	26/01/98	**
United Kingdom	26/11/87	24/06/88	09/12/93	11/04/96	09/12/93	11/04/96

* Date of signature of the convention by the Czech and Slovak Federal Republic.

** = State whose ratification is necessary for the entry into force of the protocol.

171

Framework Convention for the Protection of National Minorities

and related texts

Framework Convention for the Protection of National Minorities
(European Treaty Series, No. 157)

Strasbourg, I.II.1995

The member States of the Council of Europe and the other States, signatories to the present framework Convention,

Considering that the aim of the Council of Europe is to achieve greater unity between its members for the purpose of safeguarding and realising the ideals and principles which are their common heritage;

Considering that one of the methods by which that aim is to be pursued is the maintenance and further realisation of human rights and fundamental freedoms;

Wishing to follow-up the Declaration of the Heads of State and Government of the member States of the Council of Europe adopted in Vienna on 9 October 1993;

Being resolved to protect within their respective territories the existence of national minorities;

Considering that the upheavals of European history have shown that the protection of national minorities is essential to stability, democratic security and peace in this continent;

Considering that a pluralist and genuinely democratic society should not only respect the ethnic, cultural, linguistic and religious identity of each person belonging to a national minority, but also create appropriate conditions enabling them to express, preserve and develop this identity;

Considering that the creation of a climate of tolerance and dialogue is necessary to enable cultural diversity to be a source and a factor, not of division, but of enrichment for each society;

Considering that the realisation of a tolerant and prosperous Europe does not depend solely on co-operation between States but also requires transfrontier co-operation between local and regional authorities without prejudice to the constitution and territorial integrity of each State;

Having regard to the Convention for the Protection of Human Rights and Fundamental Freedoms and the Protocols thereto;

Having regard to the commitments concerning the protection of national minorities in United Nations conventions and declarations and in the documents of the Conference on Security and Co-operation in Europe, particularly the Copenhagen Document of 29 June 1990;

Being resolved to define the principles to be respected and the obligations which flow from them, in order to ensure, in the member States and such other States as may become Parties to the present instrument, the effective protection of national minorities and of the rights and freedoms of persons belonging to those minorities, within the rule of law, respecting the territorial integrity and national sovereignty of states;

Being determined to implement the principles set out in this framework Convention through national legislation and appropriate governmental policies,

Have agreed as follows:

Section I

Article 1

The protection of national minorities and of the rights and freedoms of persons belonging to those minorities forms an integral part of the international protection of human rights, and as such falls within the scope of international co-operation.

Article 2

The provisions of this framework Convention shall be applied in good faith, in a spirit of understanding and tolerance and in conformity with the principles of good neighbourliness, friendly relations and co-operation between States.

Article 3

1 Every person belonging to a national minority shall have the right freely to choose to be treated or not to be treated as such and no disadvantage shall result from this choice or from the exercise of the rights which are connected to that choice.

2 Persons belonging to national minorities may exercise the rights and enjoy the freedoms flowing from the principles enshrined in the present framework Convention individually as well as in community with others.

Section II

Article 4

1 The Parties undertake to guarantee to persons belonging to national minorities the right of equality before the law and of equal protection of the law. In this respect, any discrimination based on belonging to a national minority shall be prohibited.

2 The Parties undertake to adopt, where necessary, adequate measures in order to promote, in all areas of economic, social, political and cultural life, full and effective equality between persons belonging to a national minority and those belonging to the majority. In this respect, they shall take due account of the specific conditions of the persons belonging to national minorities.

3 The measures adopted in accordance with paragraph 2 shall not be considered to be an act of discrimination.

Article 5

1 The Parties undertake to promote the conditions necessary for persons belonging to national minorities to maintain and develop their culture, and to preserve the essential elements of their identity, namely their religion, language, traditions and cultural heritage.

2 Without prejudice to measures taken in pursuance of their general integration policy, the Parties shall refrain from policies or practices aimed at assimilation of persons belonging to national minorities against their will and shall protect these persons from any action aimed at such assimilation.

Article 6

1 The Parties shall encourage a spirit of tolerance and intercultural dialogue and take effective measures to promote mutual respect and understanding and co-operation among all persons living on their territory, irrespective of those persons' ethnic, cultural, linguistic or religious identity, in particular in the fields of education, culture and the media.

2 The Parties undertake to take appropriate measures to protect persons who may be subject to threats or acts of discrimination, hostility or violence as a result of their ethnic, cultural, linguistic or religious identity.

Article 7

The Parties shall ensure respect for the right of every person belonging to a national minority to freedom of peaceful assembly, freedom of association, freedom of expression, and freedom of thought, conscience and religion.

Article 8

The Parties undertake to recognise that every person belonging to a national minority has the right to manifest his or her religion or belief and to establish religious institutions, organisations and associations.

Article 9

1 The Parties undertake to recognise that the right to freedom of expression of every person belonging to a national minority includes freedom to hold opinions and to receive and impart information and ideas in the minority language, without interference by public authorities and regardless of frontiers. The Parties shall ensure, within the framework of their legal systems, that persons belonging to a national minority are not discriminated against in their access to the media.

2 Paragraph 1 shall not prevent Parties from requiring the licensing, without discrimination and based on objective criteria, of sound radio and television broadcasting, or cinema enterprises.

3 The Parties shall not hinder the creation and the use of printed media by persons belonging to national minorities. In the legal framework of sound radio and television broadcasting, they shall ensure, as far as possible, and taking into account the provisions of paragraph 1, that persons belonging to national minorities are granted the possibility of creating and using their own media.

4 In the framework of their legal systems, the Parties shall adopt adequate measures in order to facilitate access to the media for persons belonging to national minorities and in order to promote tolerance and permit cultural pluralism.

Article 10

1 The Parties undertake to recognise that every person belonging to a national minority has the right to use freely and without interference his or her minority language, in private and in public, orally and in writing.

2 In areas inhabited by persons belonging to national minorities traditionally or in substantial numbers, if those persons so request and where such a request corresponds to a real need, the Parties shall endeavour to ensure, as far as possible, the conditions which would make it possible to use the minority language in relations between those persons and the administrative authorities.

3 The Parties undertake to guarantee the right of every person belonging to a national minority to be informed promptly, in a language which he or she understands, of the reasons for his or her arrest, and of the nature and

cause of any accusation against him or her, and to defend himself or herself in this language, if necessary with the free assistance of an interpreter.

Article 11

1 The Parties undertake to recognise that every person belonging to a national minority has the right to use his or her surname (patronym) and first names in the minority language and the right to official recognition of them, according to modalities provided for in their legal system.

2 The Parties undertake to recognise that every person belonging to a national minority has the right to display in his or her minority language signs, inscriptions and other information of a private nature visible to the public.

3 In areas traditionally inhabited by substantial numbers of persons belonging to a national minority, the Parties shall endeavour, in the framework of their legal system, including, where appropriate, agreements with other States, and taking into account their specific conditions, to display traditional local names, street names and other topographical indications intended for the public also in the minority language when there is a sufficient demand for such indications.

Article 12

1 The Parties shall, where appropriate, take measures in the fields of education and research to foster knowledge of the culture, history, language and religion of their national minorities and of the majority.

2 In this context the Parties shall inter alia provide adequate opportunities for teacher training and access to textbooks, and facilitate contacts among students and teachers of different communities.

3 The Parties undertake to promote equal opportunities for access to education at all levels for persons belonging to national minorities.

Article 13

1 Within the framework of their education systems, the Parties shall recognise that persons belonging to a national minority have the right to set up and to manage their own private educational and training establishments.

2 The exercise of this right shall not entail any financial obligation for the Parties.

Article 14

1 The Parties undertake to recognise that every person belonging to a national minority has the right to learn his or her minority language.

2   In areas inhabited by persons belonging to national minorities traditionally or in substantial numbers, if there is sufficient demand, the Parties shall endeavour to ensure, as far as possible and within the framework of their education systems, that persons belonging to those minorities have adequate opportunities for being taught the minority language or for receiving instruction in this language.

3   Paragraph 2 of this article shall be implemented without prejudice to the learning of the official language or the teaching in this language.

Article 15

The Parties shall create the conditions necessary for the effective participation of persons belonging to national minorities in cultural, social and economic life and in public affairs, in particular those affecting them.

Article 16

The Parties shall refrain from measures which alter the proportions of the population in areas inhabited by persons belonging to national minorities and are aimed at restricting the rights and freedoms flowing from the principles enshrined in the present framework Convention.

Article 17

1   The Parties undertake not to interfere with the right of persons belonging to national minorities to establish and maintain free and peaceful contacts across frontiers with persons lawfully staying in other States, in particular those with whom they share an ethnic, cultural, linguistic or religious identity, or a common cultural heritage.

2   The Parties undertake not to interfere with the right of persons belonging to national minorities to participate in the activities of non-governmental organisations, both at the national and international levels.

Article 18

1   The Parties shall endeavour to conclude, where necessary, bilateral and multilateral agreements with other States, in particular neighbouring States, in order to ensure the protection of persons belonging to the national minorities concerned.

2   Where relevant, the Parties shall take measures to encourage transfrontier co-operation.

Article 19

The Parties undertake to respect and implement the principles enshrined in the present framework Convention making, where necessary, only those limitations, restrictions or derogations which are provided for in international legal instruments, in particular the Convention for the Protection of Human Rights and Fundamental Freedoms, in so far as they are relevant to the rights and freedoms flowing from the said principles.

Section III

Article 20

In the exercise of the rights and freedoms flowing from the principles enshrined in the present framework Convention, any person belonging to a national minority shall respect the national legislation and the rights of others, in particular those of persons belonging to the majority or to other national minorities.

Article 21

Nothing in the present framework Convention shall be interpreted as implying any right to engage in any activity or perform any act contrary to the fundamental principles of international law and in particular of the sovereign equality, territorial integrity and political independence of States.

Article 22

Nothing in the present framework Convention shall be construed as limiting or derogating from any of the human rights and fundamental freedoms which may be ensured under the laws of any Contracting Party or under any other agreement to which it is a Party.

Article 23

The rights and freedoms flowing from the principles enshrined in the present framework Convention, in so far as they are the subject of a corresponding provision in the Convention for the Protection of Human Rights and Fundamental Freedoms or in the Protocols thereto, shall be understood so as to conform to the latter provisions.

Section IV

Article 24

1 The Committee of Ministers of the Council of Europe shall monitor the implementation of this framework Convention by the Contracting Parties.

2 The Parties which are not members of the Council of Europe shall participate in the implementation mechanism, according to modalities to be determined.

Article 25

1 Within a period of one year following the entry into force of this framework Convention in respect of a Contracting Party, the latter shall transmit to the Secretary General of the Council of Europe full information on the legislative and other measures taken to give effect to the principles set out in this framework Convention.

2 Thereafter, each Party shall transmit to the Secretary General on a periodical basis and whenever the Committee of Ministers so requests any further information of relevance to the implementation of this framework Convention.

3 The Secretary General shall forward to the Committee of Ministers the information transmitted under the terms of this Article.

Article 26

1 In evaluating the adequacy of the measures taken by the Parties to give effect to the principles set out in this framework Convention the Committee of Ministers shall be assisted by an advisory committee, the members of which shall have recognised expertise in the field of the protection of national minorities.

2 The composition of this advisory committee and its procedure shall be determined by the Committee of Ministers within a period of one year following the entry into force of this framework Convention.

Section V

Article 27

This framework Convention shall be open for signature by the member States of the Council of Europe. Up until the date when the Convention enters into force, it shall also be open for signature by any other State so invited by the Committee of Ministers. It is subject to ratification, acceptance or approval. Instruments of ratification, acceptance or approval shall be deposited with the Secretary General of the Council of Europe.

Article 28

1 This framework Convention shall enter into force on the first day of the month following the expiration of a period of three months after the date on which twelve member States of the Council of Europe have expressed their consent to be bound by the Convention in accordance with the provisions of Article 27.

2 In respect of any member State which subsequently expresses its consent to be bound by it, the framework Convention shall enter into force on the

first day of the month following the expiration of a period of three months after the date of the deposit of the instrument of ratification, acceptance or approval.

Article 29

1 After the entry into force of this framework Convention and after consulting the Contracting States, the Committee of Ministers of the Council of Europe may invite to accede to the Convention, by a decision taken by the majority provided for in Article 20.d of the Statute of the Council of Europe, any non-member State of the Council of Europe which, invited to sign in accordance with the provisions of Article 27, has not yet done so, and any other non-member State.

2 In respect of any acceding State, the framework Convention shall enter into force on the first day of the month following the expiration of a period of three months after the date of the deposit of the instrument of accession with the Secretary General of the Council of Europe.

Article 30

1 Any State may at the time of signature or when depositing its instrument of ratification, acceptance, approval or accession, specify the territory or territories for whose international relations it is responsible to which this framework Convention shall apply.

2 Any State may at any later date, by a declaration addressed to the Secretary General of the Council of Europe, extend the application of this framework Convention to any other territory specified in the declaration. In respect of such territory the framework Convention shall enter into force on the first day of the month following the expiration of a period of three months after the date of receipt of such declaration by the Secretary General.

3 Any declaration made under the two preceding paragraphs may, in respect of any territory specified in such declaration, be withdrawn by a notification addressed to the Secretary General. The withdrawal shall become effective on the first day of the month following the expiration of a period of three months after the date of receipt of such notification by the Secretary General.

Article 31

1 Any Party may at any time denounce this framework Convention by means of a notification addressed to the Secretary General of the Council of Europe.

2 Such denunciation shall become effective on the first day of the month following the expiration of a period of six months after the date of receipt of the notification by the Secretary General.

Article 32

The Secretary General of the Council of Europe shall notify the member States of the Council, other signatory States and any State which has acceded to this framework Convention, of:

a any signature;

b the deposit of any instrument of ratification, acceptance, approval or accession;

c any date of entry into force of this framework Convention in accordance with Articles 28, 29 and 30;

d any other act, notification or communication relating to this framework Convention.

In witness whereof the undersigned, being duly authorised thereto, have signed this framework Convention.

Done at Strasbourg, this 1st day of February 1995, in English and French, both texts being equally authentic, in a single copy which shall be deposited in the archives of the Council of Europe. The Secretary General of the Council of Europe shall transmit certified copies to each member State of the Council of Europe and to any State invited to sign or accede to this framework Convention.

Explanatory report to the Framework Convention for the Protection of National Minorities

Background

1   The Council of Europe has examined the situation of national minorities on a number of occasions over a period of more than forty years. In its very first year of existence (1949), the Parliamentary Assembly recognised, in a report of its Committee on Legal and Administrative Questions, the importance of "the problem of wider protection of the rights of national minorities". In 1961, the Assembly recommended the inclusion of an article in a second additional protocol to guarantee to national minorities certain rights not covered by the European Convention on Human Rights (ECHR). The latter simply refers to "association with a national minority" in the non-discrimination clause provided for in Article 14. Recommendation 285 (1961) proposed the following wording for the draft article on the protection of national minorities:

"Persons belonging to a national minority shall not be denied the right, in community with the other members of their group, and as far as compatible with public order, to enjoy their own culture, to use their own language, to establish their schools and receive teaching in the language of their choice or to profess and practise their own religion."

2   The committee of experts, which had been instructed to consider whether it was possible and advisable to draw up such a protocol, adjourned its activities until a final decision had been reached on the Belgian linguistics cases concerning the language used in education (European Court of Human Rights, Judgment of 27 July 1968, Series A No. 6). In 1973 it concluded that, from a legal point of view, there was no special need to make the rights of minorities the subject of a further protocol to the ECHR. However, the experts considered that there was no major legal obstacle to the adoption of such a protocol if it were considered advisable for other reasons.

3   More recently, the Parliamentary Assembly recommended a number of political and legal measures to the Committee of Ministers, in particular the drawing up of a protocol or a convention on the rights of national minorities. Recommendation 1134 (1990) contains a list of principles which the Assembly considered necessary for the protection of national minorities. In October 1991, the Steering Committee for Human Rights (CDDH) was given the task of considering, from both a legal and a political point of view, the conditions in which the Council of Europe could undertake an activity for the protection

of national minorities, taking into account the work done by the Conference on Security and Co-operation in Europe (CSCE) and the United Nations, and the reflections within the Council of Europe.

4   In May 1992, the Committee of Ministers instructed the CDDH to examine the possibility of formulating specific legal standards relating to the protection of national minorities. To this end, the CDDH established a committee of experts (DH-MIN) which, under new terms of reference issued in March 1993, was required to propose specific legal standards in this area, bearing in mind the principle of complementarity of work between the Council of Europe and the CSCE. The CDDH and the

DH-MIN took various texts into account, in particular the proposal for a European Convention for the Protection of National Minorities drawn up by the European Commission for Democracy through Law (the so-called Venice Commission), the Austrian proposal for an additional protocol to the ECHR, the draft additional protocol to the ECHR included in Assembly Recommendation 1201 (1993) and other proposals. This examination culminated in the report of the CDDH to the Committee of Ministers of 8 September 1993, which included various legal standards which might be adopted in this area and the legal instruments in which they could be laid down. In this connection, the CDDH noted that there was no consensus on the interpretation of the term "national minorities".

5   The decisive step was taken when the Heads of State and Government of the Council of Europe's member States met in Vienna at the summit of 8 and 9 October 1993. There, it was agreed that the national minorities which the upheavals of history have established in Europe had to be protected and respected as a contribution to peace and stability. In particular, the Heads of State and Government decided to enter into legal commitments regarding the protection of national minorities. Appendix II of the Vienna Declaration instructed the Committee of Ministers:

–   to draft with minimum delay a framework convention specifying the principles which contracting States commit themselves to respect, in order to assure the protection of national minorities. This instrument would also be open for signature by non-member States;

–   to begin work on drafting a protocol complementing the European Convention on Human Rights in the cultural field by provisions guaranteeing individual rights, in particular for persons belonging to national minorities.

6   On 4 November 1993, the Committee of Ministers established an *ad hoc* Committee for the Protection of National Minorities (CAHMIN). Its terms of reference reflected the decisions taken in Vienna. The committee, made up of experts from the Council of Europe's member States, started work in late January 1994, with the participation of representatives of the CDDH, the

Council for Cultural Co-operation (CDCC), the Steering Committee on the Mass Media (CDMM) and the European Commission for Democracy through Law. The High Commissioner on National Minorities of the CSCE and the Commission of the European Communities also took part, as observers.

7 On 15 April 1994, CAHMIN submitted an interim report to the Committee of Ministers, which was then communicated to the Parliamentary Assembly (Doc. 7109). At its 94th session in May 1994, the Committee of Ministers expressed satisfaction with the progress achieved under the terms of reference flowing from the Vienna Declaration.

8 A certain number of provisions of the framework Convention requiring political arbitration as well as those concerning the monitoring of the implementation were drafted by the Committee of Ministers (517*bis* meeting of Ministers' Deputies, 7 October 1994).

9 At its meeting from 10 to 14 October 1994, CAHMIN decided to submit the draft framework Convention to the Committee of Ministers, which adopted the text at the 95th Ministerial Session on 10 November 1994. The framework Convention was opened for signature by the Council of Europe's member States on 1 February 1995.

General considerations

Objectives of the framework convention

10 The framework convention is the first legally binding multilateral instrument devoted to the protection of national minorities in general. Its aim is to specify the legal principles which States undertake to respect in order to ensure the protection of national minorities. The Council of Europe has thereby given effect to the Vienna Declaration's call (Appendix II) for the political commitments adopted by the Conference on Security and Co-operation in Europe (CSCE) to be transformed, to the greatest possible extent, into legal obligations.

Approaches and fundamental concepts

11 In view of the range of different situations and problems to be resolved, a choice was made for a framework Convention which contains mostly programme-type provisions setting out objectives which the Parties undertake to pursue. These provisions, which will not be directly applicable, leave the States concerned a measure of discretion in the implementation of the objectives which they have undertaken to achieve, thus enabling them to take particular circumstances into account.

12 It should also be pointed out that the framework Convention contains no definition of the notion of "national minority". It was decided to adopt a

pragmatic approach, based on the recognition that at this stage, it is impossible to arrive at a definition capable of mustering general support of all Council of Europe member States.

13 The implementation of the principles set out in this framework Convention shall be done through national legislation and appropriate governmental policies. It does not imply the recognition of collective rights. The emphasis is placed on the protection of persons belonging to national minorities, who may exercise their rights individually and in community with others (see Article 3, paragraph 2). In this respect, the framework Convention follows the approach of texts adopted by other international organisations.

Structure of the framework Convention

14 Apart from its Preamble, the framework Convention contains an operative part which is divided into five sections.

15 Section I contains provisions which, in a general fashion, stipulate certain fundamental principles which may serve to elucidate the other substantive provisions of the framework Convention.

16 Section II contains a catalogue of specific principles.

17 Section III contains various provisions concerning the interpretation and application of the framework Convention.

18 Section IV contains provisions on the monitoring of the implementation of the framework Convention.

19 Section V contains the final clauses which are based on the model final clauses for conventions and agreements concluded within the Council of Europe.

Commentary on the provisions of the framework Convention

Preamble

20 The Preamble sets out the reasons for drawing up this framework Convention and explains certain basic concerns of its drafters. The opening words already indicate that this instrument may be signed and ratified by States not members of the Council of Europe (see Articles 27 and 29).

21 The Preamble refers to the statutory aim of the Council of Europe and to one of the methods by which this aim is to be pursued: the maintenance and further realisation of human rights and fundamental freedoms.

22 Reference is also made to the Vienna Declaration of Heads of State and Government of the member States of the Council of Europe, a document which laid the foundation for the present framework Convention (see also paragraph 5 above). In fact, the text of the Preamble is largely inspired by

that declaration, in particular its Appendix II. The same is true of the choice of undertakings included in Sections I and II of the framework Convention.

23 The Preamble mentions, in a non-exhaustive way, three further sources of inspiration for the content of the framework Convention: the Convention for the Protection of Human Rights and Fundamental Freedoms (ECHR) and instruments which contain commitments regarding the protection of national minorities of the United Nations and the CSCE.

24 The Preamble reflects the concern of the Council of Europe and its member States about the risk to the existence of national minorities and is inspired by Article 1, paragraph 1, of the United Nations Declaration on the Rights of Persons belonging to National or Ethnic, Religious and Linguistic Minorities (Resolution 47/135 adopted by the General Assembly on 18 December 1992).

25 Given that the framework Convention is also open to States which are not members of the Council of Europe, and to ensure a more comprehensive approach, it was decided to include certain principles from which flow rights and freedoms which are already guaranteed in the ECHR or in the protocols thereto (see also in connection with this, Article 23 of the framework Convention).

26 The reference to United Nations conventions and declarations recalls the work done at the universal level, for example in the International Covenant on Civil and Political Rights (Article 27) and in the Declaration on the Rights of Persons belonging to National or Ethnic, Religious and Linguistic Minorities. However this reference does not extend to any definition of a national minority which may be contained in these texts.

27 The reference to the relevant CSCE commitments reflects the desire expressed in Appendix II of the Vienna Declaration that the Council of Europe should apply itself to transforming, to the greatest possible extent, these political commitments into legal obligations. The Copenhagen Document in particular provided guidance for drafting the framework Convention.

28 The penultimate paragraph in the Preamble sets out the main aim of the framework Convention: to ensure the effective protection of national minorities and of the rights of persons belonging to those minorities. It also stresses that this effective protection should be ensured within the rule of law, respecting the territorial integrity and national sovereignty of States.

29 The purpose of the last recital is to indicate that the provisions of this framework Convention are not directly applicable. It is not concerned with the law and practice of the Parties in regard to the reception of international treaties in the internal legal order.

Section I

Article 1

30 The main purpose of Article 1 is to specify that the protection of national minorities, which forms an integral part of the protection of human rights, does not fall within the reserved domain of States. The statement that this protection "forms an integral part of the international protection of human rights" does not confer any competence to interpret the present framework Convention on the organs established by the ECHR.

31 The article refers to the protection of national minorities as such and of the rights and freedoms of persons belonging to such minorities. This distinction and the difference in wording make it clear that no collective rights of national minorities are envisaged (see also the commentary to Article 3). The Parties do however recognise that protection of a national minority can be achieved through protection of the rights of individuals belonging to such a minority.

Article 2

32 This article provides a set of principles governing the application of the framework Convention. It is, *inter alia*, inspired by the United Nations Declaration on Principles of International Law concerning Friendly Relations and Co-operation among States in accordance with the Charter of the United Nations (General Assembly Resolution 2625 (XXV) of 24 October 1970). The principles mentioned in this provision are of a general nature but do have particular relevance to the field covered by the framework Convention.

Article 3

33 This article contains two distinct but related principles laid down in two different paragraphs.

Paragraph 1

34 Paragraph 1 firstly guarantees to every person belonging to a national minority the freedom to choose to be treated or not to be treated as such. This provision leaves it to every such person to decide whether or not he or she wishes to come under the protection flowing from the principles of the framework Convention.

35 This paragraph does not imply a right for an individual to choose arbitrarily to belong to any national minority. The individual's subjective choice is inseparably linked to objective criteria relevant to the person's identity.

36 Paragraph 1 further provides that no disadvantage shall arise from the free choice it guarantees, or from the exercise of the rights which are con-

nected to that choice. This part of the provision aims to secure that the enjoyment of the freedom to choose shall also not be impaired indirectly.

Paragraph 2

37 Paragraph 2 provides that the rights and freedoms flowing from the principles of the framework Convention may be exercised individually or in community with others. It thus recognises the possibility of joint exercise of those rights and freedoms, which is distinct from the notion of collective rights . The term "others" shall be understood in the widest possible sense and shall include persons belonging to the same national minority, to another national minority, or to the majority.

Section II

Article 4

38 The purpose of this article is to ensure the applicability of the principles of equality and non-discrimination for persons belonging to national minorities. The provisions of this article are to be understood in the context of this framework Convention.

Paragraphs 1 and 2

39 Paragraph 1 takes the classic approach to these principles. Paragraph 2 stresses that the promotion of full and effective equality between persons belonging to a national minority and those belonging to the majority may require the Parties to adopt special measures that take into account the specific conditions of the persons concerned. Such measures need to be "adequate", that is in conformity with the proportionality principle, in order to avoid violation of the rights of others as well as discrimination against others. This principle requires, among other things, that such measures do not extend, in time or in scope, beyond what is necessary in order to achieve the aim of full and effective equality.

40 No separate provision dealing specifically with the principle of equal opportunities has been included in the framework Convention. Such an inclusion was considered unnecessary as the principle is already implied in paragraph 2 of this article. Given the principle of non-discrimination set out in paragraph 1 the same was considered true for freedom of movement.

Paragraph 3

41 The purpose of paragraph 3 is to make clear that the measures referred to in paragraph 2 are not to be regarded as contravening the principles of equality and non-discrimination. Its aim is to ensure to persons belonging to national minorities effective equality along with persons belonging to the majority.

Article 5

42 This article essentially aims at ensuring that persons belonging to national minorities can maintain and develop their culture and preserve their identity.

Paragraph 1

43 Paragraph 1 contains an obligation to promote the necessary conditions in this respect. It lists four essential elements of the identity of a national minority. This provision does not imply that all ethnic, cultural, linguistic or religious differences necessarily lead to the creation of national minorities (see in this regard the report of the CSCE meeting of experts, held in Geneva in 1991, section II, paragraph 4).

44 The reference to "traditions" is not an endorsement or acceptance of practices which are contrary to national law or international standards. Traditional practices remain subject to limitations arising from the requirements of public order.

Paragraph 2

45 The purpose of paragraph 2 is to protect persons belonging to national minorities from assimilation against their will. It does not prohibit voluntary assimilation.

46 Paragraph 2 does not preclude the Parties from taking measures in pursuance of their general integration policy. It thus acknowledges the importance of social cohesion and reflects the desire expressed in the preamble that cultural diversity be a source and a factor, not of division, but of enrichment to each society.

Article 6

47 This article is an expression of the concerns stated in Appendix III to the Vienna Declaration (Declaration and Plan of Action on combating racism, xenophobia, anti-Semitism and intolerance).

Paragraph 1

48 Paragraph 1 stresses a spirit of tolerance and intercultural dialogue and points out the importance of the Parties' promoting mutual respect, understanding and co-operation among all who live on their territory. The fields of education, culture and the media are specifically mentioned because they are considered particularly relevant to the achievement of these aims.

49 In order to strengthen social cohesion, the aim of this paragraph is, inter alia, to promote tolerance and intercultural dialogue, by eliminating barriers between persons belonging to ethnic, cultural, linguistic and religious groups

through the encouragement of intercultural organisations and movements which seek to promote mutual respect and understanding and to integrate these persons into society whilst preserving their identity.

Paragraph 2

50 This provision is inspired by paragraph 40.2 of the Copenhagen Document of the CSCE. This obligation aims at the protection of all persons who may be subject to threats or acts of discrimination, hostility or violence, irrespective of the source of such threats or acts.

Article 7

51 The purpose of this article is to guarantee respect for the right of every person belonging to a national minority to the fundamental freedoms mentioned therein. These freedoms are of course of a universal nature, that is they apply to all persons, whether belonging to a national minority or not (see, for instance, the corresponding provisions in Articles 9, 10 and 11 of the ECHR), but they are particularly relevant for the protection of national minorities. For the reasons stated above in the commentary on the preamble, it was decided to include certain undertakings which already appear in the ECHR.

52 This provision may imply for the Parties certain positive obligations to protect the freedoms mentioned against violations which do not emanate from the State. Under the ECHR, the possibility of such positive obligations has been recognised by the European Court of Human Rights.

53 Some of the freedoms laid down in Article 7 are elaborated upon in Articles 8 and 9.

Article 8

54 This article lays down more detailed rules for the protection of freedom of religion than Article 7. It combines several elements from paragraphs 32.2, 32.3 and 32.6 of the CSCE Copenhagen Document into a single provision. This freedom of course applies to all persons and persons belonging to a national minority should, in accordance with Article 4, enjoy it as well. Given the importance of this freedom in the present context, it was felt particularly appropriate to give it special attention.

Article 9

55 This article contains more detailed rules for the protection of the freedom of expression than Article 7.

Paragraph 1

56 The first sentence of this paragraph is modelled on the second sentence of Article 10, paragraph 1, of the ECHR. Although the sentence refers specifically to the freedom to receive and impart information and ideas in the minority language, it also implies the freedom to receive and impart information and ideas in the majority or other languages.

57 The second sentence of this paragraph contains an undertaking to ensure that there is no discrimination in access to the media. The words "in the framework of their legal systems" were inserted in order to respect constitutional provisions which may limit the extent to which a Party can regulate access to the media.

Paragraph 2

58 This paragraph is modelled on the third sentence of Article 10, paragraph 1, of the ECHR.

59 The licensing of sound radio and television broadcasting, and of cinema enterprises, should be non-discriminatory and be based on objective criteria. The inclusion of these requirements, which are not expressly mentioned in the third sentence of Article 10, paragraph 1, of the ECHR, was considered important for an instrument designed to protect persons belonging to a national minority.

60 The words "sound radio", which also appear in paragraph 3 of this article, do not appear in the corresponding sentence in Article 10 of the ECHR. They are used in order to reflect modern terminology and do not imply any material difference in meaning from Article 10 of the ECHR.

Paragraph 3

61 The first sentence of this paragraph, dealing with the creation and use of printed media, contains an essentially negative undertaking whereas the more flexibly worded second sentence emphasises a positive obligation in the field of sound radio and television broadcasting (for example the allocation of frequencies). This distinction reflects the relative scarcity of available frequencies and the need for regulation in the latter field. No express reference has been made to the right of persons belonging to a national minority to seek funds for the establishment of media, as this right was considered self-evident.

Paragraph 4

62 This paragraph emphasises the need for special measures with the dual aim of facilitating access to the media for persons belonging to national minorities and promoting tolerance and cultural pluralism. The expression "adequate measures" was used for the reasons given in the commentary on

Article 4, paragraph 2 (see paragraph 39), which uses the same words. The paragraph complements the undertaking laid down in the last sentence of Article 9, paragraph 1. The measures envisaged by this paragraph could, for example, consist of funding for minority broadcasting or for programme productions dealing with minority issues and/or offering a dialogue between groups, or of encouraging, subject to editorial independence, editors and broadcasters to allow national minorities access to their media.

Article 10

Paragraph 1

63 The recognition of the right of every person belonging to a national minority to use his or her minority language freely and without interference is particularly important. The use of the minority language represents one of the principal means by which such persons can assert and preserve their identity. It also enables them to exercise their freedom of expression. "In public" means, for instance, in a public place, outside, or in the presence of other persons but is not concerned in any circumstances with relations with public authorities, the subject of paragraph 2 of this article.

Paragraph 2

64 This provision does not cover all relations between individuals belonging to national minorities and public authorities. It only extends to administrative authorities. Nevertheless, the latter must be broadly interpreted to include, for example, ombudsmen. In recognition of the possible financial, administrative, in particular in the military field, and technical difficulties associated with the use of minority languages in relations between persons belonging to national minorities and the administrative authorities, this provision has been worded very flexibly, leaving Parties a wide measure of discretion.

65 Once the two conditions in paragraph 2 are met, Parties shall endeavour to ensure the use of a minority language in relations with the administrative authorities as far as possible. The existence of a "real need" is to be assessed by the State on the basis of objective criteria. Although contracting States should make every effort to apply this principle, the wording "as far as possible" indicates that various factors, in particular the financial resources of the Party concerned, may be taken into consideration.

66 The Parties' obligations regarding the use of minority languages do not in any way affect the status of the official language or languages of the country concerned. Moreover, the framework Convention deliberately refrains from defining "areas inhabited by persons belonging to national minorities traditionally or in substantial numbers". It was considered preferable to adopt a flexible form of wording which will allow each Party's particular circumstances to be taken into account. The term "inhabited ... traditionally" does not refer to historical minorities, but only to those still living in the same

geographical area (see also Article 11, paragraph 3, and Article 14, paragraph 2).

Paragraph 3

67 This paragraph is based on certain provisions contained in Articles 5 and 6 of the European Convention on Human Rights. It does not go beyond the safeguards contained in those articles.

Article 11

Paragraph 1

68 In view of the practical implications of this obligation, the provision is worded in such a way as to enable Parties to apply it in the light of their own particular circumstances. For example, Parties may use the alphabet of their official language to write the name(s) of a person belonging to a national minority in its phonetic form. Persons who have been forced to give up their original name(s), or whose name(s) has (have) been changed by force, should be entitled to revert to it (them), subject of course to exceptions in the case of abuse of rights and changes of name(s) for fraudulent purposes. It is understood that the legal systems of the Parties will, in this respect, meet international principles concerning the protection of national minorities.

Paragraph 2

69 The obligation in this paragraph concerns an individual's right to display "in his or her minority language signs, inscriptions and other information of a private nature visible to the public". This does not, of course, exclude persons belonging to national minorities from being required to use, in addition, the official language and/or other minority languages. The expression "of a private nature" refers to all that is not official.

Paragraph 3

70 This article aims to promote the possibility of having local names, street names and other topographical indications intended for the public also in the minority language. In implementing this principle the States are entitled to take due account of the specific circumstances and the framework of their legal systems, including, where appropriate, agreements with other States. In the field covered by this provision, it is understood that the Parties are under no obligation to conclude agreements with other States. Conversely, the possibility of concluding such agreements is not ruled out. It is also understood that the legally binding nature of existing agreements remains unaffected. This provision does not imply any official recognition of local names in the minority languages.

Article 12

71 This article seeks to promote knowledge of the culture, history, language and religion of both national minorities and the majority population in an intercultural perspective (see Article 6, paragraph 1). The aim is to create a climate of tolerance and dialogue, as referred to in the preamble to the framework convention and in Appendix II of the Vienna Declaration of the Heads of State and Government. The list in the second paragraph is not exhaustive whilst the words "access to textbooks" are understood as including the publication of textbooks and their purchase in other countries. The obligation to promote equal opportunities for access to education at all levels for persons belonging to national minorities reflects a concern expressed in the Vienna Declaration.

Article 13

Paragraph 1

72 The Parties' obligation to recognise the right of persons belonging to national minorities to set up and manage their own private educational and training establishments is subject to the requirements of their educational system, particularly the regulations relating to compulsory schooling. The establishments covered by this paragraph may be subject to the same forms of supervision as other establishments, particularly with regard to teaching standards. Once the required standards are met, it is important that any qualifications awarded are officially recognised. The relevant national legislation must be based on objective criteria and conform to the principle of non-discrimination.

Paragraph 2

73 The exercise of the right referred to in paragraph 1 does not entail any financial obligation for the Party concerned, but neither does it exclude the possibility of such a contribution.

Article 14

Paragraph 1

74 The obligation to recognise the right of every person belonging to a national minority to learn his or her minority language concerns one of the principal means by which such individuals can assert and preserve their identity. There can be no exceptions to this. Without prejudice to the principles mentioned in paragraph 2, this paragraph does not imply positive action, notably of a financial nature, on the part of the State.

Paragraph 2

75 This provision concerns teaching of and instruction in a minority language. In recognition of the possible financial, administrative and technical difficulties associated with instruction of or in minority languages, this provision has been worded very flexibly, leaving Parties a wide measure of discretion. The obligation to endeavour to ensure instruction of or in minority languages is subject to several conditions; in particular, there must be "sufficient demand" from persons belonging to the relevant national minorities. The wording "as far as possible" indicates that such instruction is dependent on the available resources of the Party concerned.

76 The text deliberately refrains from defining "sufficient demand", a flexible form of wording which allows Parties to take account of their countries' own particular circumstances. Parties have a choice of means and arrangements in ensuring such instruction, taking their particular educational system into account.

77 The alternatives referred to in this paragraph – "opportunities for being taught the minority language or for receiving instruction in this language" – are not mutually exclusive. Even though Article 14, paragraph 2, imposes no obligation upon States to do both, its wording does not prevent the States Parties from implementing the teaching of the minority language as well as the instruction in the minority language. Bilingual instruction may be one of the means of achieving the objective of this provision. The obligation arising from this paragraph could be extended to pre-school education.

Paragraph 3

78 The opportunities for being taught the minority language or for receiving instruction in this language are without prejudice to the learning of the official language or the teaching in this language. Indeed, knowledge of the official language is a factor of social cohesion and integration.

79 It is for States where there is more than one official language to settle the particular questions which the implementation of this provision shall entail.

Article 15

80 This article requires Parties to create the conditions necessary for the effective participation of persons belonging to national minorities in cultural, social and economic life and in public affairs, in particular those affecting them. It aims above all to encourage real equality between persons belonging to national minorities and those forming part of the majority. In order to create the necessary conditions for such participation by persons belonging to national minorities, Parties could promote – in the framework of their constitutional systems – *inter alia* the following measures:

- consultation with these persons, by means of appropriate procedures and, in particular, through their representative institutions, when Parties are contemplating legislation or administrative measures likely to affect them directly;
- involving these persons in the preparation, implementation and assessment of national and regional development plans and programmes likely to affect them directly;
- undertaking studies, in conjunction with these persons, to assess the possible impact on them of projected development activities;
- effective participation of persons belonging to national minorities in the decision-making processes and elected bodies both at national and local levels;
- decentralised or local forms of government.

Article 16

81 The purpose of this article is to protect against measures which change the proportion of the population in areas inhabited by persons belonging to national minorities and are aimed at restricting the rights and freedoms which flow from the present framework Convention. Examples of such measures might be expropriation, evictions and expulsions or redrawing administrative borders with a view to restricting the enjoyment of such rights and freedoms ("gerrymandering").

82 The article prohibits only measures which are aimed at restricting the rights and freedoms flowing from the framework Convention. It was considered impossible to extend the prohibition to measures having the effect of restricting such rights and freedoms, since such measures may sometimes be entirely justified and legitimate. One example might be resettlement of inhabitants of a village in order to build a dam.

Article 17

83 This article contains two undertakings important to the maintenance and development of the culture of persons belonging to a national minority and to the preservation of their identity (see also Article 5, paragraph 1). The first paragraph deals with the right to establish and maintain free and peaceful contacts across frontiers, whereas the second paragraph protects the right to participate in the activities of non-governmental organisations (see also in this connection, the provisions on freedom of assembly and of association in Article 7).

84 The provisions of this article are largely based on paragraphs 32.4 and 32.6 of the Copenhagen Document of the CSCE. It was considered unnecessary to include an explicit provision on the right to establish and maintain contacts within the territory of a State, since this was felt to be adequately

covered by other provisions of the framework Convention, notably Article 7 as regards freedom of assembly and of association.

Article 18

85 This article encourages the Parties to conclude, in addition to the existing international instruments, and where the specific circumstances justify it, bilateral and multilateral agreements for the protection of national minorities. It also stimulates transfrontier co-operation. As is emphasised in the Vienna Declaration and its Appendix II, such agreements and co-operation are important for the promotion of tolerance, prosperity, stability and peace.

Paragraph 1

86 Bilateral and multilateral agreements as envisaged by this paragraph might, for instance, be concluded in the fields of culture, education and information.

Paragraph 2

87 This paragraph points out the importance of transfrontier co-operation. Exchange of information and experience between States is an important tool for the promotion of mutual understanding and confidence. In particular, transfrontier co-operation has the advantage that it allows for arrangements specifically tailored to the wishes and needs of the persons concerned.

Article 19

88 This article provides for the possibility of limitations, restrictions or derogations. When the undertakings included in this framework Convention have an equivalent in other international legal instruments, in particular the ECHR, only the limitations, restrictions or derogations provided for in those instruments are allowed. When the undertakings set forth in this framework Convention have no equivalent in other international legal instruments, the only limitations, restrictions or derogations allowed are those which, included in other legal instruments (such as the ECHR) in respect of different undertakings, are relevant.

Section III

Article 20

89 Persons belonging to national minorities are required to respect the national constitution and other national legislation. However, this reference to national legislation clearly does not entitle Parties to ignore the provisions of the framework Convention. Persons belonging to national minorities must also respect the rights of others. In this regard, reference may be made to sit-

uations where persons belonging to national minorities are in a minority nationally but form a majority within one area of the State.

Article 21

90 This provision stresses the importance of the fundamental principles of international law and specifies that the protection of persons belonging to national minorities must be in accordance with these principles.

Article 22

91 This provision, which is based on Article 60 of the ECHR, sets out a well-known principle. The aim is to ensure that persons belonging to national minorities benefit from whichever of the relevant national or international human rights legislation is most favourable to them.

Article 23

92 This provision deals with the relationship between the framework Convention and the Convention for the Protection of Human Rights and Fundamental Freedoms, reference to which is included in the Preamble. Under no circumstances can the framework Convention modify the rights and freedoms safeguarded in the Convention for the Protection of Human Rights and Fundamental Freedoms. On the contrary, rights and freedoms enshrined in the framework Convention which are the subject of a corresponding provision in the Convention for the Protection of Human Rights and Fundamental Freedoms must be interpreted in accordance with the latter.

Section IV

Articles 24-26

93 To provide for overseeing the application of the framework Convention, the Committee of Ministers is entrusted with the task of monitoring the implementation by the Contracting Parties. The Committee of Ministers shall determine the modalities for the participation in the implementation mechanism by the Parties which are not members of the Council of Europe.

94 Each Party shall transmit to the Secretary General on a periodical basis and whenever the Committee of Ministers so requests information of relevance to the implementation of this framework Convention. The Secretary General shall transmit this information to the Committee of Ministers. However, the first report, the aim of which is to provide full information on legislative and other measures which the Party has taken to give effect to the undertakings set out in the framework Convention, must be submitted within one year of the entry into force of the framework Convention in respect of the Party concerned. The purpose of the subsequent reports shall be to complement the information included in the first report.

95 In order to ensure the efficiency of the monitoring of the implementation of the framework Convention, it provides for the setting up of an advisory committee. The task of this advisory committee is to assist the Committee of Ministers when it evaluates the adequacy of the measures taken by a Party to give effect to the principles set out in the framework Convention.

96 It is up to the Committee of Ministers to determine, within one year of the entry into force of the framework Convention, the composition and the procedures of the advisory committee, the members of which shall have recognised expertise in the field of the protection of national minorities.

97 The monitoring of the implementation of this framework Convention shall, in so far as possible, be transparent. In this regard it would be advisable to envisage the publication of the reports and other texts resulting from such monitoring.

Section V

98 The final provisions contained in articles 27 to 32 are based on the model final clauses for conventions and agreements concluded within the Council of Europe. No article on reservations was included; reservations are allowed in as far as they are permitted by international law. Apart from Articles 27 and 29 the articles in this section require no particular comment.

Articles 27 and 29

99 The framework Convention is open for signature by the Council of Europe's member States and, at the invitation of the Committee of Ministers, by other States. It is understood that "other States" are those States which participate in the Conference on Security and Co-operation in Europe. These provisions take account of the Vienna Declaration, according to which the framework Convention should also be open for signature by non-member States (see Appendix II to the Vienna Declaration of the Council of Europe Summit).

Rules adopted by the Committee of Ministers on the monitoring arrangements under Articles 24 to 26 of the Framework Convention for the Protection of National Minorities

(Resolution (97) 10, adopted by the Committee of Ministers on 17 September 1997 at the 601st meeting of the Ministers' Deputies)

I The Advisory Committee provided for by Article 26 of the Framework Convention for the Protection of National Minorities: composition, election and appointment

A Membership of the Advisory Committee

1 Members

1 Members of the Advisory Committee shall be appointed in accordance with these rules. They shall sit as either ordinary or additional members.

2 The number of ordinary members of the Advisory Committee shall be a minimum of twelve and a maximum of eighteen. This shall not prohibit the Advisory Committee from commencing its work in accordance with Rule 28.

3 Members of the Advisory Committee may not be substituted.

4 There shall not be more than one member in respect of any party.

2 Qualifications and capacity of the members

5 The members of the Advisory Committee shall have recognised expertise in the field of the protection of national minorities.

6 The members of the Advisory Committee shall serve in their individual capacity, shall be independent and impartial, and shall be available to serve the committee effectively.

B Procedure for election and appointment

1 General

7 The Committee of Ministers shall elect experts to the list of experts eligible to serve on the Advisory Committee (hereafter referred to as "the list")

and appoint ordinary and additional members in accordance with the following rules.

2   Election of experts to the list

8   Each party may submit to the Secretary General the names and the curricula vitae, in one of the official languages of the Council of Europe, of at least two experts who have the required qualifications and capacity to serve on the Advisory Committee. The Secretary General shall transmit these documents to the Committee of Ministers.

9   The Committee of Ministers shall elect one of these experts and enter him/her on the list in respect of that party.

10   Elections shall be held in the chronological order in which the names and curricula vitae submitted by parties have been received.

11   The same procedure shall apply when entries on the list expire or lose their validity. For the sake of continuity, elections may be held during the six-month period preceding the expiry or loss of validity of the current entry on the list in respect of a party.

12   The entry on the list shall remain valid until one of the following cases arises:

- the expert concerned requests the Secretary General to delete his/her entry on the list;
- the Committee of Ministers finds that the expert concerned no longer has the required capacity;
- the expert concerned dies;
- the ordinary membership of the Advisory Committee of the expert concerned expires or ends in accordance with Rule 16.

13   The Secretary General shall act as the depositary of the list.

3   Ordinary members

a   Appointment of ordinary members

14   As long as the number of entries on the list does not exceed eighteen, each expert whose name has been entered on the list shall be appointed as an ordinary member of the Advisory Committee by the Committee of Ministers. Appointments shall follow the chronological order of the elections.

15   Once the number of entries on the list exceeds eighteen, the Committee of Ministers shall, in filling vacant seats in the Advisory Committee, give priority to appointing, in the following order, experts on the list from the parties in respect of which no ordinary member has been appointed:

   i   at two or more consecutive rounds of appointments immediately preceding the current one;

ii   at the round of appointments immediately preceding the current one;

followed by experts on the list from other parties in respect of which there is currently no ordinary member.

For each of these categories, the rule shall apply that if the number of experts entitled to appointment exceeds the number of vacant seats, ordinary members shall be selected by the Committee of Ministers through the drawing of lots.

b Term of office of ordinary members

16 The term of office of an ordinary member of the Advisory Committee shall be four years. The Committee of Ministers shall specify the exact date on which the term of office begins. No one may be appointed to serve as an ordinary member more than twice. Ordinary membership will end at an earlier date in the following cases:

- at the request of the ordinary member to the Secretary General;
- when the Committee of Ministers finds that an ordinary member no longer has the required capacity;
- when the ordinary member dies.

However, the initial term of office of half of the number of ordinary members as it stands two years after the commencement of work of the Advisory Committee shall be extended by two years. These members shall be identified at that time by the drawing of lots by the Committee of Ministers. They may also be re-appointed once, in accordance with the preceding paragraph.

17 In order to ensure that, as far as possible, one half of the ordinary membership of the Advisory Committee shall be renewed every two years, the Committee of Ministers may decide, before proceeding to any subsequent appointment, that the term or terms of office of one or more members to be appointed shall be for a period other than four years but not more than six and not less than two years.

18 An ordinary member appointed to fill a casual vacancy shall hold the seat for the remainder of the predecessor's term. Casual vacancies will be filled by experts entered onto the list in respect of the same party, unless the Committee of Ministers decides otherwise.

4 Additional members

19 During consideration of a state report from a party in respect of which there is no ordinary member of the Advisory Committee, the expert who is on the list in respect of that party shall be invited to sit as an additional member. The additional member shall perform his or her functions in accordance with Rules 33 and 34.

II The procedure to be followed in performing the monitoring functions

1 Transmission and publicity of state reports

20 State reports shall be transmitted by the party to the Secretary General who will transmit them to the Committee of Ministers. The state reports shall be made public by the Council of Europe upon receipt by the Secretary General, without prejudice to the right of the state to make the report public at an earlier date.

21 The periodical basis for transmission of state reports mentioned in Article 25, paragraph 2, of the framework convention is set at five years, calculated from the date on which the previous report was due.

2 Consideration of state reports by the Advisory Committee

22 The Committee of Ministers shall transmit the state reports to the Advisory Committee.

23 The Advisory Committee shall consider the state reports and shall transmit its opinions to the Committee of Ministers.

3 Consideration of state reports by the Committee of Ministers

24 Following receipt of the opinion of the Advisory Committee, the Committee of Ministers shall consider and adopt its conclusions concerning the adequacy of the measures taken by the Contracting Party concerned to give effect to the principles of the framework convention. It may also adopt recommendations in respect of the party concerned, and set a time-limit for the submission of information on their implementation.

4 Publicity

25 The conclusions and recommendations of the Committee of Ministers shall be made public upon adoption.

26 The opinion of the Advisory Committee concerning the report of a party shall be made public at the same time as the conclusions and recommendations of the Committee of Ministers, unless in a specific case the Committee of Ministers decides otherwise.

27 Comments of the parties in relation to the opinion of the Advisory Committee shall be made public together with the conclusions and recommendations of the Committee of Ministers and the opinion of the Advisory Committee.

5 Working methods of the Advisory Committee

28 The Advisory Committee shall commence its work once twelve ordinary members have been appointed, or at an earlier stage if the Committee of

Ministers so decides; and in any event not later than one year after the entry into force of the framework convention.

29 The Advisory Committee may request additional information from the party whose report is under consideration.

30 The Advisory Committee may receive information from sources other than state reports.

31 Unless otherwise directed by the Committee of Ministers, the Advisory Committee may invite information from other sources after notifying the Committee of Ministers of its intention to do so.

32 The Advisory Committee may hold meetings with representatives of the government whose report is being considered and shall hold a meeting if the government concerned so requests.

A specific mandate shall be obtained from the Committee of Ministers if the Advisory Committee wishes to hold meetings for the purpose of seeking information from other sources.

These meetings shall be held in closed session.

33 Additional members of the Advisory Committee shall only participate in the work of the Advisory Committee in respect of the report of the party in respect of which they have been elected to the list.

34 Additional members shall sit in an advisory capacity; they shall not have the right to take part in a possible vote. The same shall apply to ordinary members regarding the report of the party in respect of which they have been elected to the list.

6   Ad hoc *reports*

35 The Advisory Committee may invite the Committee of Ministers to request an *ad hoc* report from a party.

7   *Follow-up*

36 The Advisory Committee shall be involved in the monitoring of the follow-up to the conclusions and recommendations on an *ad hoc* basis, as instructed by the Committee of Ministers.

8   *Rules of procedure and periodic reports*

37 The Advisory Committee shall draft its rules of procedure which shall be submitted to the Committee of Ministers for approval. The same procedure shall apply to any subsequent modification to the rules of procedure.

38 The Advisory Committee shall periodically inform the Committee of Ministers on the state of its work.

III Participation in the Committee of Ministers by parties which are not members of the Council of Europe

39 The Committee of Ministers shall invite a representative from each non-member Party to attend the meetings of the Committee of Ministers – without the right to participate in the adoption of decisions – whenever it exercises its functions under the framework convention.

Framework Convention for the Protection of National Minorities: signatures and ratifications at 1 January 1999

Member states	Framework Convention	
	Signed	Ratified
Albania	29/06/95	—
Andorra	—	—
Austria	01/02/95	31/03/98
Belgium	—	—
Bulgaria	09/10/97	—
Croatia	06/11/96	11/10/97
Cyprus	01/02/95	04/06/96
Czech Republic	28/04/95	18/12/97
Denmark	01/02/95	22/09/97
Estonia	02/02/95	06/01/97
Finland	01/02/95	03/10/97
France	—	—
Germany	11/05/95	10/09/97
Greece	22/09/97	—
Hungary	01/02/95	25/09/95
Iceland	01/02/95	—
Ireland	01/02/95	—
Italy	01/02/95	03/11/97
Latvia	11/05/95	—
Liechtenstein	01/02/95	18/11/97
Lithuania	01/02/95	—
Luxembourg	20/07/95	—
Malta	11/05/95	10/02/98
Moldova	13/07/95	20/11/96
Netherlands	01/02/95	—
Norway	01/02/95	—
Poland	01/02/95	—
Portugal	01/02/95	—
Romania	01/02/95	11/05/95
Russian Federation	28/02/96	21/08/98
San Marino	11/05/95	05/12/96
Slovakia	01/02/95	14/09/95
Slovenia	01/02/95	25/03/98
Spain	01/02/95	01/09/95
Sweden	01/02/95	—
Switzerland	01/02/95	21/10/98
"The former Yugoslav Republic of Macedonia"	25/07/96	10/04/97
Turkey	—	—
Ukraine	15/09/95	26/01/98
United Kingdom	01/02/95	15/01/98

Non-member state

Armenia	25/07/97	20/07/98

The Framework Convention is open for signature by the member states and by any other state so invited by the Committee of Ministers.

Sales agents for publications of the Council of Europe
Agents de vente des publications du Conseil de l'Europe